★ ★ ★

HISTORIC AMERICAN COVERED BRIDGES

BRIAN J. McKEE

ASCE PRESS

AMERICAN SOCIETY OF CIVIL ENGINEERS
345 EAST 47TH STREET, NEW YORK NY 10017

OXFORD UNIVERSITY PRESS
198 MADISON AVENUE, NEW YORK NY 10016

1997

Abstract

Covered wooden bridges are a visual testament to the American spirit. Originally designed with roof-like "covers" to protect the exposed wood from the effects of sun and rain, these bridges became treasured gathering places in rural America for events from political rallies to weddings.

One of the most extensive photographic records covering 138 selected historic covered bridges found in North America, the book offers detailed truss diagrams, basic construction details, and location information for each featured bridge. A complete index of all of the nearly 1,000 surviving covered bridges is included.

A number of bridges are presented in multipage formats: The Medora and Williams Bridges are two of the longest covered bridges left in the United States. Kentucky's Bennett Mill Bridge is the only surviving Wheeler truss bridge. The Stark Bridge in New Hampshire provides one of the most picturesque scenes in America, with the little white Union Church sitting by its side. The Roberts Bridge is the only remaining double-barreled covered bridge in Ohio and only one of six remaining in the United States. The Parker Bridge, also located in Ohio, was nearly destroyed by a fire in 1991, but after a fundraising drive, its restoration was completed in 1992.

Library of Congress Cataloging-in-Publication Data

McKee, Brian J.
Historic American covered bridges / Brian J. McKee.
p.   cm.
ISBN 0-7844-0189-6 / ISBN 0-19-521335-1
1. Covered bridges—United States. 2. Historic bridges—United States.   I. Title.
TG23.M34 1996   96-26724
624'.3'0973—dc20   CIP

The material presented in this publication has been prepared in accordance with generally recognized engineering principles and practices, and is for general information only. This information should not be used without first securing competent advice with respect to its suitability for any general or specific application.

The contents of this publication are not intended to be and should not be construed to be a standard of the American Society of Civil Engineers (ASCE) and are not intended for use as a reference in purchase specifications, contracts, regulations, statutes, or any other legal document.

No reference made in this publication to any specific method, product, process or service constitutes or implies an endorsement, recommendation, or warranty thereof by ASCE.

ASCE makes no representation or warranty of any kind, whether express or implied, concerning the accuracy, completeness, suitability, or utility of any information, apparatus, product, or process discussed in this publication, and assumes no liability therefore.

Anyone utilizing this information assumes all liability arising from such use, including but not limited to infringement of any patent or patents.

Cover photo by Brian J. McKee: Humpback/Geer's Mill Bridge, Vinton County, OH
Interior design by Vincent Gatti

Library of Congress Catalog Card No: 96-26724
ISBN 0-7844-0189-6 / ISBN 0-19-521335-1
Printed in Hong Kong.
Co-published by Oxford University Press, inc. 198 Madison Avenue New York NY 10016

To Katie,

MY WONDERFUL DAUGHTER WHO HAS TRAVELED TO MORE COVERED BRIDGES WITH ME THAN SHE CARES TO REMEMBER, AND ALSO TO ALL OF MY GOOD FRIENDS WHOM I HAVE MET ALONG THE NARROW BACK ROADS THAT LEAD TO THE HISTORIC COVERED BRIDGE.

COVERED BRIDGE ORGANIZATIONS The following organizations are instrumental in the preservation and documentation of the timber covered bridge and have members from around the world. All of the listed groups publish informative newsletters and some have monthly or bi-monthly meetings. You are encouraged to write to them for more information.

OHIO HISTORIC BRIDGE ASSOCIATION
3155 WHITEHEAD ROAD, COLUMBUS, OH 43204

THEODORE BURR COVERED BRIDGE
SOCIETY OF PENNSYLVANIA
P. O. BOX 2383, LANCASTER, PA 17603-2383

INDIANA COVERED BRIDGE SOCIETY
725 SANDERS STREET, INDIANAPOLIS, IN 46203

KENTUCKY COVERED BRIDGE ASSOCIATION
62 MIAMI PARKWAY, FORT THOMAS, KY 41075-1137

NEW YORK STATE COVERED BRIDGE SOCIETY
958 GROVE STREET, ELMIRA, NY 14901

NATIONAL SOCIETY FOR
THE PRESERVATION OF COVERED BRIDGES
52 SAMOSET VILLAGE, ROCKPORT, ME 04856

OREGON COVERED BRIDGE SOCIETY
14595 SW NEILL ROAD, SHERWOOD, OR 97140

SOCIÉTÉ QUÉBÉCOISE DES PONTS
COUVERTS, INC. (SQPC)
2126 DELORIMIER, LONGUEUIL, QC J4K 3N9

THE BRIDGE COVERED
110 SHADY LANE, FAYETTEVILLE, NY 13066

CONTENTS

PREFACE
VII

ACKNOWLEDGMENTS
VIII

INTRODUCTION
I

SOURCES
3

PREFACE

I WAS INTRODUCED TO THE WORLD OF COVERED BRIDGES ON A COLD EVENING IN DECEMBER OF 1976, WHEN I CAME ACROSS THE PARKER BRIDGE IN WYANDOT COUNTY, OHIO, A LONG, DARK RED BRIDGE SITTING IN A QUIET VALLEY OF A RURAL FARMING COMMUNITY, UNTOUCHED BY MODERN REINFORCEMENTS AND MODIFICATIONS. HAD IT NOT BEEN FOR A 2 TON LOAD LIMIT SIGN IN FRONT OF IT, I WOULD HAVE THOUGHT THAT I WAS ENTERING SOMEONE'S GARAGE, FOR I HAD NEVER SEEN A COVERED BRIDGE BEFORE. FIFTEEN YEARS LATER, I DECIDED TO REVISIT IT AND TAKE A FEW PHOTOS WITH MY NEW CAMERA, BUT NOT LONG AFTER THIS SECOND ENCOUNTER, THE PARKER BRIDGE WAS NEARLY DESTROYED BY ARSONISTS. PHOTOGRAPHING ALL OF THEM THAT I COULD FIND BECAME BOTH AN URGENT MISSION AND AN ENJOYABLE PASTIME FOR ME AND I BEGAN TO MEET OTHERS WHO HAD THE SAME INTEREST. SOME OF THESE PEOPLE HAVE BECOME MY CLOSEST FRIENDS, AND WE KEEP IN CONSTANT TOUCH. IN JULY OF 1995, I WAS ASKED BY MARY GRACE LUKE, BOOK ACQUISITIONS EDITOR OF ASCE PRESS, TO WRITE A BOOK ABOUT HISTORIC COVERED BRIDGES. NATURALLY, I WAS DELIGHTED WITH THE OPPORTUNITY TO HAVE SOME OF MY

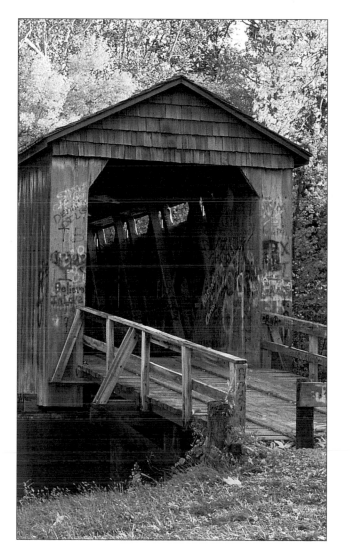

MANY PHOTOGRAPHS OF THE OLD COVERED BRIDGES IN PRINT, AND ALSO TO SHARE THIS OPPORTUNITY WITH SEVERAL OF MY GOOD FRIENDS WHO ARE EQUALLY DEDICATED TO THE PRESERVATION OF THE WOODEN TRUSS COVERED BRIDGE. THESE FRIENDS RESPONDED QUITE ENTHUSIASTICALLY WHEN I ASKED THEM TO SUBMIT SOME OF THEIR OUTSTANDING PHOTOS FOR THE BOOK, AND FOR THIS I AM VERY GRATEFUL TO THEM.

SINCE 1991, I HAVE BEEN INTENSIVELY PURSUING THE REMAINING OLD COVERED BRIDGES AROUND THE EASTERN UNITED STATES, SEEKING THEM OUT TO PHOTOGRAPH AND COLLECT INFORMATION ABOUT THEM WHICH I STORE IN MY MACINTOSH COMPUTER. THIS INFORMATION WAS QUITE HELPFUL IN THE PREPARATION OF THIS BOOK, ALTHOUGH THERE IS STILL A LACK OF GOOD, PRECISE DATA ABOUT MANY OF THE BRIDGES BECAUSE MOST OF THEM WERE BUILT SO LONG AGO.

MY SLIDES HAVE BEEN A PART OF MANY COMMUNITY PROGRAMS AND I ALWAYS ENJOY SPEAKING TO GROUPS ABOUT MY HOBBY. EVEN THOSE WHO ARE TOTALLY UNFAMILIAR WITH THE COVERED BRIDGE FIND THESE PROGRAMS INTERESTING AND USUALLY HAVE LOTS OF QUESTIONS AFTERWARDS. OF COURSE, THE MORE AWARE THE PUBLIC IS MADE OF THE HISTORIC IMPORTANCE OF COVERED BRIDGES, THE MORE LIKELY THEY WILL BE PRESERVED FOR FUTURE GENERATIONS TO ENJOY.

ORIGINALLY, MY INTENTION WAS TO WRITE A BOOK THAT WOULD INCLUDE PHOTOS OF ALL THE EXISTING COVERED BRIDGES IN NORTH AMERICA, NUMBERING SLIGHTLY OVER 1000, BUT DUE TO BUDGET CONSTRAINTS, THIS COULD NOT BE ACCOMPLISHED, SO I HAVE CHOSEN WHAT I FEEL ARE THE MOST SIGNIFICANT STRUCTURES FOR USE IN THIS PUBLICATION. I REALIZE THAT SOME WILL QUESTION MY CHOICES AND WONDER WHY I LEFT CERTAIN BRIDGES OUT, BUT I HAVE MANY REASONS FOR SELECTING THE ONES THAT I DID. NEVERTHELESS, CHOOSING THEM WAS UNDOUBTEDLY THE MOST DIFFICULT TASK IN THIS PROJECT.

I HOPE THAT THOSE WHO ARE ALREADY FAMILIAR WITH THE COVERED BRIDGE AND ITS PLACE IN AMERICAN HISTORY WILL NOT FIND THIS BOOK TOO REDUNDANT AND WILL AT LEAST ENJOY THE PHOTOGRAPHS. FOR THE NEWCOMER WHO HAS JUST PICKED UP THIS BOOK, I WOULD ENCOURAGE YOU TO DRIVE (OR BICYCLE) TO A FEW OF THE BRIDGES AND SEE FOR YOURSELF WHAT FASCINATING SUBJECTS THEY ARE. JOIN A COVERED BRIDGE ORGANIZATION AND READ THEIR NEWSLETTERS TO FIND OUT MORE ABOUT THEM. WHO KNOWS, MAYBE IT WILL BE THE BEGINNING OF A VERY FULFILLING NEW PASTIME, AND YOU MAY EVEN MEET SOME NEW FRIENDS ALONG THE WAY.

ACKNOWLEDGMENTS

My sincere appreciation and gratitude is reserved for the following people who have unselfishly given their photos and other important information to me for use in this project.

Gérald Arbour,
President, Société québécoise des ponts couverts, inc.

Rick Bray,
who edited the Indiana section of the bridge index

Roger and Christy Tolle,
owners of Marion Photo Finishers who process my film

Richard T. Donovan,
photographer/historian

Thomas Hildreth, photographer

Mary Grace Luke, Acquisitions Editor, who has been my main contact with ASCE Press throughout the project

Rodney and Connie Nolder, photographers

Philip Pierce of Binghamton, New York, for spending many hours proofreading the main text of the book

Jeffrey M. Reichard, photographer

Joanne C. Schmitz, photographer

Thomas E. Walczak, President, Theodore Burr Covered Bridge Society of Pennsylvania

Richard Wilson, President, New York State Covered Bridge Society

Shima Yoshio, photographer/writer

Also, thank you to Susan Sarver and Suzanne White of the ASCE offices in Washington, D.C., who organized an exhibition of my photos in their building in 1995, which ultimately led to the idea for this book.

A special thanks goes out to my dear friend Mr. Richard T. Donovan, of Milton, Pennsylvania, who not only provided photos, but enthusiastically spent many hours proofreading and correcting the hundreds of errors in the text and list of bridges. Mr. Donovan has studied covered bridges for the past 40 years and has the most complete set of records and maps regarding them in existence. In 1980, he edited the World Guide to Covered Bridges, a publication still used by many "bridgers." Were it not for his help and encouragement over the years, this book simply wouldn't have been written.

INTRODUCTION

At the turn of the nineteenth century, the covered bridge began its life in the United States and quickly became the most common way for travelers to cross the thousands of rivers, streams, and gullies that had hindered their progress in the past. The first covered bridge on record is the Permanent Bridge, which was built in 1805 in Philadelphia by Timothy Palmer, a Massachusetts bridge builder. It was covered with siding and a roof to protect its expensive trusses from the damaging effects of the weather. This method of bridge construction soon caught on with other inventors and builders, and therefore became the rage in the new bridge building industry.

During the first 50 years of the nineteenth century, wooden covered bridges were built by the thousands, mainly in the eastern U.S. This fury of construction continued, but gradually slowed after the British inventor Sir Henry Bessemer introduced his new steel smelting process in 1855. The Bessemer process allowed steel to be produced cheaply and therefore was competitive with wood as a construction material. The fact that steel bridges wouldn't burn presented yet another very strong argument for choosing them over wooden ones.

Some covered bridges were made with combinations of wood and steel components, such as the Howe, Pratt, and Post trusses. These designs raised the load capacity of the bridge considerably, and were favorites of the railroad industry.

By the late nineteenth century, the wooden bridge was almost forgotten, except in the western U.S. and Canada. Steel had taken over as the preferred bridge building material. Occasionally, a few new ones are built for nostalgic reasons or where there is considerable corrosion damage to steel and concrete bridges due to the usage of salt on the roadways in the winter. Wooden bridges are unaffected by those same corrosive effects, and some reports show that they may actually be preserved by the salt.

The number of these wooden bridges in North America has dwindled down to about 1000 due to several factors. First, they have become obsolete in this day of high-speed modern traffic. Their narrow openings and single lane design (in most cases) create a bottleneck in traffic that is unacceptable on all but the most infrequently used roads. Replacing them with wider concrete bridges is a commonly used solu-

tion to traffic problems. Second, they are subject to destruction due to fire, flooding, high winds, and overloaded vehicles. Many were burnt during the Civil War to keep the enemy from crossing the river. Third, they are lost to decay and neglect. If they are not maintained occasionally, they will soon rot and collapse. By keeping the roof and siding in good condition, they seem to last indefinitely.

Covered bridge enthusiasts known as "bridgers" are a unique group of people who are attracted to them for several quite different reasons, the first of which is their rustic charm and beauty. There is nothing quite like driving down a seldom used dirt road and discovering an old covered bridge quietly sitting in the valley, awaiting its next passenger. Its presence makes one pause and ponder the type of lifestyle that existed in the colonial era, when horse-drawn vehicles were the only mode of transportation. As one enters the bridge, the fragrance of its aging wood triggers thoughts of log cabins and barns, which are also becoming extinct throughout the American landscape. Countless couples have found that the covered bridge provides an ideal romantic atmosphere in which to steal a kiss, thereby giving them the common nickname "kissing bridges."

Historians are especially interested in the old covered bridges because of their important role in the development of the early American transportation system. Many bridges were built near a mill to facilitate access to it from both sides of the river. As more bridges were built, the goods and services produced in a certain community were more readily available to those in neighboring communities. Travelers were no longer hindered by raging rivers and slow, inconvenient ferry boats. Tolls were often collected as a means to pay for and maintain the bridge, and a toll house was sometimes part of the bridge design.

Engineers may look at the covered bridge from yet another perspective, that of the truss design. Without the wooden truss system, there would never have been a covered bridge in the first place. These trusses allowed bridges to span wide rivers without having to support them with piers, which were often washed away in floods. Men designed new trusses and patented them so that they could sell their designs by the foot for a profit. Some became wealthy as a result, and others didn't. Many men who were skilled carpenters and stone masons were employed by the bridge companies to work long, hard hours under

STRENUOUS, UNPLEASANT CONDITIONS. KEEP IN MIND THAT THERE WERE NO POWER TOOLS, NO AUTOMOBILES, AND NO PLACE TO ESCAPE THE HOT SUMMER TEMPERATURES. TIMBERS WERE SHAPED WITH SPECIAL AXES, CHISELS, AND KNIVES WITHOUT THE AID OF ELECTRICITY. STILL, DESPITE THE MANY HARDSHIPS OF CONSTRUCTING TIMBER BRIDGES IN THE REMOTE AREAS OF THE COUNTRY, THESE MEN PERFORMED THEIR WORK WITH QUALITY AND PRECISION THAT IS ALMOST UNHEARD OF TODAY. THE FACT THAT SO MANY COVERED BRIDGES ARE STILL BEING USED ON A DAILY BASIS IS A TESTAMENT TO THESE MEN AND THEIR FINE WORK.

FORTUNATELY, IT IS NO LONGER CONSIDERED PRACTICAL TO DESTROY AN OLD COVERED BRIDGE JUST BECAUSE IT HAS BECOME A NUISANCE OR BOTTLENECK TO MODERN TRAFFIC. MOST ENGINEERS NOW REALIZE THEIR HISTORICAL SIGNIFICANCE AND MAKE AN EFFORT TO SAVE AN OLD BRIDGE IN SOME MANNER, EVEN IF IT MEANS MOVING IT TO A PARK TO SIT AS A MONUMENT.

COVERED BRIDGE "PURISTS" ARE OUTRAGED TO SEE ANY MODIFICATIONS DONE TO AN OLD BRIDGE, AND TO THEM IT IS UNACCEPTABLE TO ALTER THE FLOOR OR ANY OTHER PART OF THE BRIDGE FROM ITS ORIGINAL DESIGN. I SHARE THEIR CONCERNS IN THIS AREA; HOWEVER, IT IS NOT PRACTICAL TO THINK THAT ALL OF THE REMAINING OLD COVERED BRIDGES CAN BE PRESERVED IN AN UNALTERED STATE FOR THE NEXT SEVERAL CENTURIES, ESPECIALLY IF THEY ARE ASKED TO CARRY LARGE AMOUNTS OF MODERN TRAFFIC ON A DAILY BASIS. BYPASSING THEM WITH A NEW CONCRETE OR IRON BRIDGE IS ONE SOLUTION TO PRESERVING THEM, BUT THIS USUALLY LEADS TO THEIR NEGLECT AND EVENTUAL DEMISE AT THE HANDS OF VANDALS OR MOTHER NATURE. LEAVING A BYPASSED COVERED BRIDGE OPEN TO TRAFFIC MAY BE AN ACCEPTABLE WAY TO KEEP IT MAINTAINED, AND AT THE SAME TIME REDUCE THE TRAFFIC LOAD THAT IT IS REQUIRED TO CARRY, AS IS DONE IN A COUPLE OF EXAMPLES IN ASHTABULA COUNTY, OHIO, AND IN NEW JERSEY.

THERE ARE SEVERAL COVERED BRIDGE ORGANIZATIONS THAT SERVE TO PROVIDE THEIR MEMBERS WITH CURRENT INFORMATION ABOUT THE BRIDGES AND RELATED SUBJECTS THROUGH NEWSLETTERS, AND ALSO TO PROMOTE THEIR PRESERVATION. MOST OF THEM HOLD MONTHLY OR BI-MONTHLY MEETINGS AND TOURS. THERE IS A LIST OF THESE ORGANIZATIONS ELSEWHERE IN THIS BOOK.

I HAVE RESTRICTED THE SELECTION OF BRIDGES FOR THIS BOOK TO ONLY AUTHENTIC WOODEN TRUSS STRUCTURES AND NOT THE "STRINGER" TYPE BRIDGE, WHICH DOES NOT RELY ON A TRUSS FOR ITS SUPPORT. THE BRIDGES THAT ARE INCLUDED RANGE FROM THE OLDEST, LONGEST, AND MOST UNIQUE DESIGN, AND OTHERS MAY HAVE AN INTERESTING HISTORICAL BACKGROUND. SOME FOLKS LIKE THE STRINGER BRIDGES FOR THEIR CHARMING APPEARANCE, AND INDEED THERE ARE SOME VERY WELL BUILT ONES AROUND THE COUNTRY, BUT THEY ARE NOT APPROPRIATE FOR THIS PUBLICATION. THERE ARE ALSO SEVERAL BRIDGES THAT SEEM TO BE A HYBRID COMBINATION OF AUTHENTIC AND STRINGER TYPE DESIGN, ONE OF WHICH IS THE GREAT PHILIPPI BRIDGE IN PHILIPPI, WEST VIRGINIA, SITE OF THE FIRST LAND BATTLE OF THE CIVIL WAR. IT RETAINS ITS ORIGINAL TRUSS SYSTEM, BUT THE OLD WOODEN FLOOR HAS BEEN REPLACED WITH CONCRETE AND STEEL TO SUPPORT THE TREMENDOUS AMOUNT OF HEAVY MODERN TRAFFIC THAT TRAVELS THROUGH IT ON US 250.

IN THIS BOOK, I HAVE LISTED WHAT I BELIEVE TO BE THE MOST RELIABLE DATA ABOUT THE BRIDGES, BUT REALIZE THAT SOME OF IT JUST MIGHT BE INACCURATE OR UNVERIFIABLE. AS I SEARCHED THROUGH MY COLLECTION OF MANY PUBLICATIONS ABOUT COVERED BRIDGES, I WAS AMAZED AT THE DIFFERENT STATISTICS FOR THE SAME BRIDGE AND ULTIMATELY HAD TO CHOOSE WHAT I THOUGHT WERE THE BEST DATA. MAINLY SPEAKING, I AM REFERRING TO THE DATE OF CONSTRUCTION AND THE LENGTH OF THE BRIDGES. LENGTH, OF COURSE, CAN BE MEASURED AT ANY TIME, BUT DATES OF CONSTRUCTION ARE VERY DIFFICULT TO VERIFY. ONLY RECENTLY HAVE I BEEN MEASURING THE BRIDGES WITH A 200 FT SURVEYOR'S TAPE. MY LENGTHS ARE MEASURED ALONG THE FLOOR LEVEL, FROM ONE PORTAL TO THE OTHER, AND DO NOT TAKE INTO ACCOUNT ANY ROOF OVERHANG. THIS MAY BE ONE EXPLANATION FOR SOME OF THE DIFFERENCES BETWEEN MY READINGS AND THOSE OF OTHERS.

THE ONLY WAY TO PROVE THE ACTUAL DATES OF CONSTRUCTION OF AN OLD BRIDGE IS TO FIND THE ORIGINAL ORDER OR BID FOR CONSTRUCTION IN COUNTY JOURNALS OR PERHAPS AN OLD NEWSPAPER ARTICLE. THIS PROCESS IS VERY TIME CONSUMING AND REQUIRES SOMEONE WITH PATIENCE AND A GOOD KNOWLEDGE OF RESEARCH PROCEDURES, SUCH AS MIRIAM WOOD, HISTORIAN AND CHARTER MEMBER OF THE OHIO HISTORIC BRIDGE ASSOCIATION. AS TIME GOES ON, MORE ACCURATE DATA ABOUT THE BRIDGES ARE UNCOVERED AND ENTERED INTO THE RECORDS, SO THE INFORMATION IS CONSTANTLY CHANGING AND BEING UPDATED.

ONE PUBLICATION THAT I MUST RECOMMEND IS THE "WORLD GUIDE TO COVERED BRIDGES" BY THE NATIONAL SOCIETY FOR THE PRESERVATION OF COVERED BRIDGES, INC. IT LISTS ALL EXISTING AUTHENTIC COVERED BRIDGES IN THE WORLD AND THEIR GENERAL STATISTICS ALONG WITH DIRECTIONS TO EACH OF THEM. IT HAS BEEN REVISED SEVERAL TIMES AND IS SCHEDULED TO BE REPRINTED WITH UPDATES IN LATE 1996. IT CAN BE PURCHASED BY WRITING TO IRENE EBERHARDT, 1257 WORCHESTER RD. #136, FRAMINGHAM, MA 01701. AT THIS TIME, THE COST IS $8.00, BUT THAT IS SUBJECT TO CHANGE.

FOR THOSE OF YOU WHO DECIDE TO SEEK OUT SOME OF THESE OLD BRIDGES, I ADVISE YOU TO PURCHASE SOME OF THE MAPS THAT ARE LISTED IN THE BIBLIOGRAPHY OF THIS BOOK. THEY WILL BE INVALUABLE IN YOUR QUEST TO FIND THE BRIDGES WITHIN A REASONABLE AMOUNT OF TIME. IF YOU STILL HAVE TROUBLE LOCATING A BRIDGE, JUST DROP ME A LETTER AT P.O. BOX 321, MARION, OH 43301-0321, AND I WILL BE GLAD TO ASSIST YOU.

SOURCES

BOOKS

ALLEN, RICHARD SANDERS. COVERED BRIDGES OF THE MIDDLE ATLANTIC STATES.
BRATTLEBORO, VT. THE STEPHEN GREENE PRESS. 1959

ALLEN, RICHARD SANDERS. COVERED BRIDGES OF THE NORTHEAST.
BRATTLEBORO, VT. THE STEPHEN GREENE PRESS. 1957

ALLEN, RICHARD SANDERS. COVERED BRIDGES OF THE SOUTH.
BRATTLEBORO, VT. THE STEPHEN GREENE PRESS. 1970

ALLEN, RICHARD SANDERS. COVERED BRIDGES OF THE MIDDLE WEST.
BRATTLEBORO, VT. THE STEPHEN GREENE PRESS. 1970

ARBOUR, GÉRALD. LES PONTS ROUGES DU QUÉBEC.
ST-EUSTACHE, QC. SOCIÉTÉ QUÉBÉCOISE DES PONTS COUVERTS, INC. 1988

COCKRELL, NICK AND BILL. ROOFS OVER RIVERS.
BEAVERTON, OR. THE TOUCHSTONE PRESS. 1978

COHEN, JOSEPH S. WORLD GUIDE TO COVERED BRIDGES.
THE NATIONAL SOCIETY FOR THE PRESERVATION OF COVERED BRIDGES, INC. 1996

COHEN, STAN. WEST VIRGINIA'S COVERED BRIDGES, A PICTORIAL HERITAGE.
CHARLESTON, WV. PICTORIAL HISTORIES PUBLISHING CO., INC. 1992

DONOVAN, RICHARD T. WORLD GUIDE TO COVERED BRIDGES.
THE NATIONAL SOCIETY FOR THE PRESERVATION OF COVERED BRIDGES, INC. 1980

EVANS, BENJAMIN D. AND JUNE R. PENNSYLVANIA'S COVERED BRIDGES, A COMPLETE
GUIDE. PITTSBURGH, PA THE UNIVERSITY OF PITTSBURGH PRESS. 1993

FRENCH, EDWARD L. AND THOMAS L., JR. COVERED BRIDGES OF GEORGIA.
COLUMBUS, GA. THE FRENCO COMPANY. 1984

HELSEL, BILL. WORLD GUIDE TO COVERED BRIDGES. MARLBORO, MA.
THE NATIONAL SOCIETY FOR THE PRESERVATION OF COVERED BRIDGES. 1989

HOWARD, ANDREW R. COVERED BRIDGES OF MASSACHUSETTS, A GUIDE.
UNIONVILLE, CT. THE VILLAGE PRESS. 1995

KETCHAM, BRYAN E. COVERED BRIDGES ON THE BYWAYS OF INDIANA.
OXFORD, OH. OXFORD PRINTING CO. 1949

KREKELER, BRENDA. COVERED BRIDGES TODAY. CANTON, OH. DARING BOOKS. 1989

MARSHALL, RICHARD G. NEW HAMPSHIRE COVERED BRIDGES...A LINK WITH OUR
PAST. NASHUA, NH. NEW HAMPSHIRE DEPARTMENT OF TRANSPORTATION. 1994

ROBERTSON, EDWIN AND DORIS K. MAINE COVERED BRIDGE FINDER.
WESTBROOK, ME. EDWIN B. ROBERTSON. 1995

SANGSTER, TOM AND DESS L. ALABAMA'S COVERED BRIDGES.
MONTGOMERY, AL. COFFEETABLE PUBLICATIONS. 1980

WOOD, MIRIAM. THE COVERED BRIDGES OF OHIO, AN ATLAS AND HISTORY.
COLUMBUS, OH. SELF PUBLISHED. 1993

ZACHER, SUSAN. THE COVERED BRIDGES OF PENNSYLVANIA. HARRISBURG, PA.
THE PENNSYLVANIA HISTORIC AND MUSEUM COMMISSION. 1989

MAPS

INDIANA COUNTY MAPS. LYNDON STATION, WI. COUNTY MAPS,
THOMAS PUBLICATIONS, LTD.

INDIANA COVERED BRIDGE LOCATION GUIDE.
THE INDIANA COVERED BRIDGE SOCIETY; ARTHUR GATEWOOD, JR. 1988

KENTUCKY COUNTY MAPS. LYNDON STATION, WI.
COUNTY MAPS, THOMAS PUBLICATIONS, LTD.

MAINE ATLAS AND GAZETTEER. FREEPORT, ME. DELORME MAPPING CO.

MICHIGAN ATLAS AND GAZETTEER. FREEPORT, ME. DELORME MAPPING CO. 1989

MICHIGAN COUNTY MAPS. LYNDON STATION, WI.
COUNTY MAPS, THOMAS PUBLICATIONS, LTD.

NEW HAMPSHIRE ATLAS AND GAZETTEER. FREEPORT, ME. DELORME MAPPING CO. 1988

NEW YORK STATE ATLAS AND GAZETTEER. FREEPORT, ME. DELORME MAPPING CO. 1991

OHIO ATLAS AND GAZETTEER. FREEPORT, ME. DELORME MAPPING CO. 1991

OHIO COUNTY MAPS. LYNDON STATION, WI.
COUNTY MAPS, THOMAS PUBLICATIONS, LTD.

OHIO HISTORIC BRIDGE GUIDE. THE OHIO HISTORIC BRIDGE ASSOCIATION. 1993

OREGON ATLAS AND GAZETTEER. FREEPORT, ME. DELORME MAPPING CO. 1991

PENNSYLVANIA ATLAS AND GAZETTEER. FREEPORT, ME. DELORME MAPPING CO. 1990

PENNSYLVANIA COUNTY MAPS. LYNDON STATION, WI.
COUNTY MAPS, THOMAS PUBLICATIONS, LTD.

TENNESSEE COUNTY MAPS. LYNDON STATION, WI.
COUNTY MAPS, THOMAS PUBLICATIONS, LTD.

VERMONT ATLAS AND GAZETTEER. FREEPORT, ME. DELORME MAPPING CO. 1988

VIRGINIA ATLAS AND GAZETTEER. FREEPORT, ME. DELORME MAPPING CO. 1989

WASHINGTON ATLAS AND GAZETTEER. FREEPORT, ME. DELORME MAPPING CO. 1995

WEST VIRGINIA COUNTY MAPS. LYNDON STATION, WI.
COUNTY MAPS, THOMAS PUBLICATIONS, LTD.

PERIODICALS

COVERED BRIDGE TOPICS. THE NATIONAL SOCIETY FOR THE PRESERVATION OF
COVERED BRIDGES. VOL. LIII NO. 3; SUMMER 1995

COVERED BRIDGE TOPICS. THE NATIONAL SOCIETY FOR THE PRESERVATION OF
COVERED BRIDGES. VOL. LIII NO. 4; FALL 1995

EMPIRE STATE COURIER. THE NEW YORK STATE COVERED BRIDGE SOCIETY. MARCH 1976

EMPIRE STATE COURIER. THE NEW YORK STATE COVERED BRIDGE SOCIETY.
NOVEMBER 1984

EMPIRE STATE COURIER. THE NEW YORK STATE COVERED BRIDGE SOCIETY. MARCH 1991

EMPIRE STATE COURIER. THE NEW YORK STATE COVERED BRIDGE SOCIETY.
VOL. 27, NO. 3; NOVEMBER 1992

EMPIRE STATE COURIER. THE NEW YORK STATE COVERED BRIDGE SOCIETY. MARCH 1995

CHATEAUGUAY VALLEY HISTORICAL SOCIETY ANNUAL JOURNAL.
THE POWERSCOURT COVERED BRIDGE. HOWICK, QC. VOL. 22; 1989

SWANN/JOY BRIDGE

Measuring 324 feet in length, the Swann/Joy Bridge is the longest remaining wooden covered bridge in the southern U.S. It was built by Zelma Tidwell high above the Locust Fork of the Black Warrior River with an impressive triple-span Town lattice truss system supported by two concrete piers. Extensive repairs were done on the bridge in 1979, and today it remains open to automobile traffic. The bridge is located a half mile west of Cleveland, just west of Route 79.

TOWN TRUSS

1933, W.G. No. 01-05-05
BLOUNT COUNTY, ALABAMA
PHOTO BY RICHARD T. DONOVAN

TOWN TRUSS

1934, W.G. No. 01-05-07
BLOUNT COUNTY, ALABAMA
PHOTO BY SHIMA YOSHIO

HORTON'S MILL BRIDGE

Horton's Mill Bridge is the third-longest covered bridge in the southern U.S. with its 220 foot long Town lattice truss. It crosses the Calvert Prong of the Black Warrior River with two spans, and sits about 70 feet above the river bed, giving it the distinction of being the highest covered bridge above water in North America. It was constructed by Zelma Tidwell to provide a route to T.M. Horton's Mill. In 1974 the bridge was restored and listed on the National Register of Historic Places. It is located about 5 miles north of Oneonta on the west side of SR75.

CLARKSON/LEGG BRIDGE

The second-longest covered bridge in the southern U.S. crosses the Crooked Creek with a 270 foot two-span Town lattice truss. It was built in 1904, repaired extensively in 1922 after a flood damaged it, then completely restored in 1975 by Ivan Williams. The last restoration included new stone piers that extend 45 feet above the riverbed. Today, it is closed to automobile traffic and bypassed with a modern bridge. It is located about 8 miles west of Cullman on CR53 at a park accompanied by an old grist mill. In 1974, the Clarkson Bridge was named to the National Register of Historic Places.

TOWN TRUSS

1904, W.G. No. 01-22-01
CULLMAN COUNTY, ALABAMA
PHOTO BY SHIMA YOSHIO

The Honey Run Bridge was built in 1896 using the Pratt truss and king post. The three-span structure crosses the Butte Creek with a length of 230 feet and is closed to today's modern traffic. The center span of the bridge has a noticeably higher roof level than the end spans, giving the Honey Run Bridge a one-of-a-kind appearance. It is located about 8 miles east of Chico on Honey Run Road.

HONEY RUN BRIDGE

1896, W.G. No. 05-04-01
BUTTE COUNTY, CALIFORNIA
PHOTO BY SHIMA YOSHIO

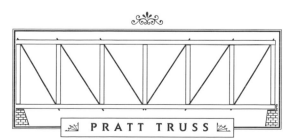

PRATT TRUSS

Bridgeport Bridge

The Bridgeport Bridge, sometimes known as "Wood's Crossing," is well known to bridge experts because it is one of the two longest remaining single-span covered bridges in the world. At 233 feet, it is slightly shorter that the Blenheim Bridge in New York. It uses a combination of Howe truss and wooden arch to support it across the South Fork of the Yuba River. The arch can be seen from the outside of the bridge, giving it a unique appearance. Built in 1862 by David I. Wood, it is presently closed to modern traffic, and it has been bypassed by a new bridge. It is one of only three covered bridges to be designated a National Historic Civil Engineering Landmark. Its location is northwest of Nevada City on Pleasant Valley Road.

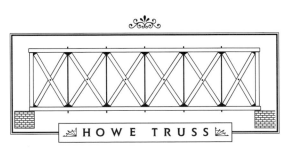

HOWE TRUSS

1862, W.G. No. 05-29-01
NEVADA COUNTY, CALIFORNIA
PHOTO BY SHIMA YOSHIO

KNIGHT'S FERRY BRIDGE

HOWE TRUSS

1864, W.G. No. 05-50-01
STANISLAUS COUNTY, CALIFORNIA
PHOTO BY SHIMA YOSHIO

At 330 feet, the Knight's Ferry Bridge is the longest covered bridge west of the Mississippi River. It was built in 1864 with the Howe truss system and uses four spans to cross the Stanislaus River. Originally operated as a private toll bridge, it was purchased by Stanislaus county in 1884. It is located at the south edge of Knight's Ferry, which is along CA108/120, and has been closed to automobile traffic since 1981.

Bull's Bridge was built in 1842 and crosses the Housatonic River just west of US7 on Bull's Bridge Road. It measures 109 feet in length and is constructed with a single span utilizing both the Town and queen-post trusses. When the photo was taken in 1994, the bridge was being restored.

BULL'S BRIDGE

1842, W.G. NO. 07-03-01
LITCHFIELD COUNTY, CONNECTICUT
PHOTO BY BRIAN J. MCKEE

TOWN

TRUSS

TOWN TRUSS

1841, W.G. No. 07-03-02
LITCHFIELD COUNTY, CONNECTICUT
PHOTO BY BRIAN J. McKEE

WEST CORNWALL BRIDGE

Built in 1841, the West Cornwall Bridge carries a tremendous amount of traffic to and from the charming town of West Cornwall, which is located just east of US7 on CT128. It uses both queen-post and Town lattice trusses to cross the Housatonic River with two spans and measures 242 feet long, making it Connecticut's longest remaining covered bridge. One unusual feature of the West Cornwall Bridge is that it has glass windowpanes, whereas most covered bridges have open windows.

The Ashland Bridge is one of only two remaining historic covered bridges in Delaware. It crosses the Red Clay Creek with its 52 foot long single-span Town lattice truss. It was built around 1870 and is located on Brackenville Road, ESE of Yorklyn.

ASHLAND BRIDGE

c1870, W.G. No. 08-02-02
NEW CASTLE COUNTY, DELAWARE
PHOTO BY BRIAN J. McKEE

TOWN

TRUSS

TOWN TRUSS

1886, W.G. No. 10-08-01
BARTOW COUNTY, GEORGIA
PHOTO BY SHIMA YOSHIO

LOWRY BRIDGE

The Lowry Bridge was built in 1886 using the Town lattice truss system. Named after the Lowry Mill that was nearby, it spans the Euharlee Creek with a length of 138 feet and sits on stone piers. There is a long wooden approach at each end of the bridge. No longer used for automobile traffic, it can still be admired as it sits quietly along the east side of Covered Bridge Road near Stilesboro.

Concord/Ruff's Mill Bridge

When the Concord/Ruff's Mill Bridge was built in 1872, its builders probably never dreamed that it would carry the thousands of vehicles per day that it does across the Nickajack Creek. It was originally constructed by Martin L. Ruff and Robert Daniell using two queen-post trusses supported in the center with a stone pier. It measures 132 feet long. Two more piers were added sometime during the 1950s, along with steel I-beams to give the bridge floor a higher load capacity. The two men also built a dam and mill nearby that still stand today.

QUEEN TRUSS

1872, W.G. No. 10-33-02
COBB COUNTY, GEORGIA
PHOTO BY RICHARD T. DONOVAN

The Coheelee Creek Bridge was constructed in 1891 by J.W. Baughman and J.B. Mosley at McDonald's Ford and has the distinction of being the southernmost covered bridge remaining in the United States today. Its modified queen-post trusses span the creek with a length of 120 feet and use a center pier for additional support. It is located northwest of Hilton on Old River Road in a park area.

COHEELEE CREEK BRIDGE

1891, W.G. No. 10-49-02
EARLY COUNTY, GEORGIA
PHOTO BY SHIMA YOSHIO

QUEEN

TRUSS

WATSON MILL BRIDGE

The beautiful Watson Mill Bridge uses three spans to cross the South Fork of the Broad River, tying the two counties together. Built in c1885 by Washington W. King, it measures 228 feet long and uses the Town lattice truss system. In the late 1800s, there were several types of mills next to it, one of which was owned by Gabriel Watson. None of the old mills remain today. It is located in the Watson Mill State Park, which is about 11 miles east of GA72 on GA22.

TOWN

TRUSS

c1885, W.G. No. 10-97-01
MADISON-OGLETHORPE COUNTIES, GEORGIA
PHOTO BY SHIMA YOSHIO

The Red Bridge crosses the Big Bureau Creek with a 93 foot long single-span Howe truss system. It has a cedar shake roof and red vertical siding that completely covers the bridge without any windows or ventilation openings. There are steel I-beam approach spans at each end of the bridge and short steel guard railings. The Red Bridge still carries automobile traffic as it has for the past 133 years. It lies 2 miles northwest of Princeton on Old Dixon-Princeton Road.

Text on bridge sign: FIVE DOLLARS FINE FOR DRIVING MORE THAN TWELVE HORSES MULES OR CATTLE AT ONE TIME OR FOR LEADING ANY BEAST FASTER THAN A WALK ON OR ACROSS THIS BRIDGE

HOWE TRUSS

RED BRIDGE

1863, W.G. No. 13-06-01
BUREAU COUNTY, ILLINOIS
PHOTO BY THOMAS E. WALCZAK

Burr Truss

Allaman/Eames Bridge

1866, W.G. No. 13-36-01

Henderson County, Illinois

Photo by Shima Yoshio

The Allaman or Eames Bridge was built in 1866 by Jacob Allman for $2125. He used the Burr truss system to span the Henderson Creek with the 106 foot long bridge, which served the public until 1934. After that, it was bypassed and remained part of a roadside park. In 1982, a flood washed it from its abutments and a group of local citizens were able to salvage the remains to have it rebuilt two years later by Ray Shafer of Biggsville. It is located north of Gladstone in a park along the east side of IL164.

LITTLE MARY'S RIVER BRIDGE

Little Mary's River Bridge is the oldest remaining covered bridge in the state of Illinois, having been constructed in 1854. It uses the Burr truss system and crosses the Little Mary's River with a single span of 98 feet. The cut stone abutments and parapets give it a feeling of great strength while the wooden shake roof lends to its rustic look. Closed to automobile traffic in 1930, it originally was on a wooden toll road between Breman and Chester. Today, it is part of a park area on the east side of IL50, northeast of Chester.

1854, W.G. No. 13-79-01
RANDOLPH COUNTY, ILLINOIS
PHOTO BY SHIMA YOSHIO

19

The Thompson Mill Bridge was built in 1868 for $2500 using the Howe truss system, and crosses the Kaskaskia River with a single span. Measuring 105 feet long, it sits on two concrete and steel piers with wooden approach ramps leading to each end. The name comes from the owner of the first mill that was nearby. Bypassed and closed, today it is located about 3.5 miles northeast of Cowden.

THOMPSON MILL BRIDGE

1868, W.G. No. 13-87-01
SHELBY COUNTY, ILLINOIS
PHOTO BY SHIMA YOSHIO

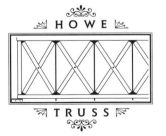

HOWE

TRUSS

This remotely located bridge is seldom used, but it still has the charm and intrigue that make covered bridges irresistible. It has a rare version of the Howe truss that uses a single wooden diagonal compression member and an iron rod for the tension member. A normal Howe truss has an additional wooden element. The bridge is 60 feet long and has a 30 foot long wooden approach at the north end. Originally built in 1880 by P. Hutti of Kentucky, it was restored extensively in 1982 and is still open to the public. It is only a few minutes north of Nashville on CR135W.

BEAN BLOSSOM BRIDGE

1880, W.G. No. 14-07-01
BROWN COUNTY, INDIANA
PHOTO BY BRIAN J. MCKEE

HOWE TRUSS

On the bridge:

1838

HENRY WOLF. BUILDER

USE RIGHT LANE ONLY   CLEARANCE 9' 0"

9 FT. CLEARANCE

BURR
TRUSS

1838, W.G. No. 14-07-02
BROWN COUNTY, INDIANA
PHOTO BY BRIAN J. MCKEE

RAMP CREEK BRIDGE

Indiana's only remaining double-barreled covered bridge carries a tremendous amount of traffic in and out of the Brown County State Park, which is near the interesting town of Nashville. In 1932, it was moved to its present location from the original site near Fincastle in Putnam County. The bridge is made from a triple set of Burr arch trusses in which one of them is placed down the center of the bridge in order to provide greater strength. Only six such bridges survive in the U.S., although they were once a rather common site. Ramp Creek Bridge was built by Aaron Wolfe in 1838, making it Indiana's oldest covered bridge. It spans the Salt Creek with a length of 96 feet.

WESTPORT BRIDGE

The Westport Bridge is no longer used for automobile traffic since being bypassed in 1975, but is still appreciated by countless fishermen and bicyclists as they need to cross the Sand Creek. A.M. Kennedy and Sons of Rush County built the Westport Bridge in 1880 using a 115 foot long Burr truss system, as they did in most of their bridges. It sits on massive stone abutments that are in excellent condition. There is a full-length window with a roof over it on each side of the bridge to provide light and ventilation. It is located on CR100S on the southeast edge of Westport, just off Main Street.

1880, W.G. No. 14-16-01
DECATUR COUNTY, INDIANA
PHOTO BY BRIAN J. MCKEE

The Whitewater Canal Aqueduct is the only surviving covered bridge of this type in the country, and fortunately has been preserved by the Whitewater Canal Association for historical purposes. It was built to carry water for the Whitewater Canal across the Duck Creek in the town of Metamora. Sitting on cut stone abutments, it has a length of 81 feet and a single-span Burr truss design. It was extensively rebuilt in 1946 through 1949, then restored again in 1991-1992. The historic town of Metamora attracts thousands of visitors every year to its old shops and old water-driven flour mill. Visitors can also take a ride through the bridge on a canal boat when in season. Metamora is located on US52, about 1 mile east of IN229 in Metamora Township.

WHITEWATER CANAL AQUEDUCT

1846, W.G. No. 14-24-11
FRANKLIN COUNTY, INDIANA
PHOTO BY BRIAN J. McKEE

BURR

TRUSS

Bell's Ford Bridge is one of three outstanding covered bridges in Jackson County, and has the distinction of being the only surviving post truss covered bridge in the world. The trusses are a most interesting combination of wood and steel members and are unique to this structure. It was built by the Seymour Bridge Company with two spans resting on cut stone abutments and a stone center pier. Closed and bypassed, the 325 foot bridge crosses the East Fork of the White River, and joins Hamilton and Jackson Townships. At the time of this writing, the bridge was being straightened with wire rope and turnbuckles fastened diagonally on the inside of the structure. Hopefully, it will be preserved so that others may enjoy this one-of-a-kind engineering masterpiece. Visitors can find Bell's Ford Bridge 2.5 miles west of Seymour on the north side of IN258.

BELL'S FORD BRIDGE

1869, W.G. No. 14-36-03
JACKSON COUNTY, INDIANA
PHOTO BY BRIAN J. MCKEE

POST TRUSS

MEDORA BRIDGE

Depending on how it is measured, the Medora Bridge could be the nation's longest existing covered bridge. A tape laid along the floor from end to end will show a length of 460 feet, which is 10 feet longer than the Cornish-Windsor Bridge when measured in this manner. Measuring along the roof would no doubt give the edge to the Cornish-Windsor Bridge, however. Medora Bridge was constructed in 1875 by J.J. Daniels with a three-span Burr truss system and is supported by stone abutments and two stone piers. Bypassed and closed to traffic, it sits undisturbed across the East Fork of the White River, joining Carr and Driftwood Townships. People can't miss this outstanding structure as they travel along IN235 east of Medora.

1875, W.G. No. 14-36-04
JACKSON COUNTY, INDIANA
PHOTO BY BRIAN J. McKEE

BURR
TRUSS

WILLIAMS BRIDGE

The Williams Bridge has the distinction of being Indiana's longest covered bridge still in use, and ranks second longest in the U.S. in this respect. Measuring 397 feet in length, it is a remarkable sight as it sits high above the East Fork of the White River. Hugh cut stone abutments and a center pier support the two-span Howe truss structure, which shows no signs of sagging. One resource gives the builder as J.J. Daniels and another gives credit to the Massillon Bridge Company in Ohio. It was restored in 1984 and is listed on the National Register of Historic Places. Williams Bridge is located in Spice Valley Township, 1 mile west of Williams on IN450, then left on CR000W.

1884, W.G. No. 14-47-02
LAWRENCE COUNTY, INDIANA
PHOTO BY BRIAN J. MCKEE

BURR
TRUSS

MANSFIELD BRIDGE

The Mansfield Bridge is located at the village of Mansfield, Indiana, which also boasts having one of the finest historic mills in the state, the Mansfield Roller Mill. A visit to this town is like stepping back in time. It was common in the nineteenth century to have a covered bridge near a mill, since both were related to the river and were very important to the success of the community. The bridge was built by Joseph J. Daniels over the Big Racoon Creek at a cost of $12,200. It is an impressive 279 foot long two-span Burr truss structure which rests on cut limestone abutments and a center pier of the same material. The red vertical siding and white portals are typical of many of Parke County's 33 covered bridges. The bridge is well cared for by the Parke County Highway Department and should last for a good many years to come.

BURR TRUSS

1867, W.G. No. 14-61-20
PARKE COUNTY, INDIANA
PHOTO BY BRIAN J. McKEE

WEST UNION BRIDGE

One of 33 covered bridges remaining in Parke County, the West Union Bridge is the longest at 335 feet. It crosses the Sugar Creek with two spans using the Burr truss system. Famed covered bridge contractor J.J. Daniels built the West Union Bridge in 1876. Although bypassed and no longer open to traffic, it still serves as a popular attraction in the county, especially during the Covered Bridge Festival held each October. It is located on CR525W, about a half mile north of West Union.

The Jackson Bridge is Indiana's longest single-span covered bridge at 207 feet, and the nation's longest single-span covered bridge that is still open to traffic. It is an outstanding example of the Burr truss system, which was used extensively in Indiana and Pennsylvania. Famed bridge builder J.J. Daniels originally constructed the Jackson Bridge with his trademark quality and attention to detail. The bridge is one of 33 covered bridges in Parke County , and one of two that span the Sugar Creek. It is located in Penn Township, west of the Turkey Run State Park on CR550W.

JACKSON BRIDGE

1861, W.G. No. 14-61-28
PARKE COUNTY, INDIANA
PHOTO BY BRIAN J. MCKEE

BURR TRUSS

HOWE TRUSS

1880, W.G. No. 14-67-13
PUTNAM COUNTY, INDIANA
PHOTO BY BRIAN J. McKEE

DICK HUFFMAN BRIDGE

Of the nine remaining covered bridges in Putnam County, the Dick Huffman Bridge is both the oldest and the longest. Named for a neighboring landowner, it was built with a two-span Howe truss system and measures 273 feet long. It still carries traffic over the Big Walnut Creek and sits on two cut stone abutments and a center pier. It shares the same dark red paint and vertical wood siding with the other covered bridges in the county, all of which seem to be kept in good working condition. The Dick Huffman Bridge can be located in Washington Township about 3 miles south of Pleasant Gardens, and just north of I-70, on CR1050S.

The Moscow Bridge is found in the small village of Moscow, Indiana, and is typical of the style of covered bridges built by the famous Kennedy family from Rushville. This particular bridge was built by Emmett L. Kennedy using the two-span Burr truss system to cross the Big Flat Rock River. It measures 335 feet in length and has a single cut stone center pier. The bridge is well maintained and is used quite often by both automobile traffic and the numerous Amish that live nearby. Moscow Bridge is the longest surviving Kennedy-built bridge and the longest covered bridge in Rush County. Its great height above the riverbed and the long, narrow windows make a breathtaking side view.

MOSCOW BRIDGE

1886, W.G. No. 14-70-07
RUSH COUNTY, INDIANA
PHOTO BY BRIAN J. McKEE

BURR

TRUSS

Roann Bridge

1872, W.G. No. 14-85-01
Wabash County, Indiana
Photo by Brian J. McKee

HOWE TRUSS

The Roann Bridge is a massive Howe truss structure that uses two spans to cross the Eel River in this small northern Indiana town. Not only is it very long at 288 feet, but it has an 18 foot clearance height and is 16 feet wide. It was constructed by the Smith Bridge Company of Toledo, Ohio, builders of many covered bridges in Indiana, Ohio, and Pennsylvania. Tragedy struck in September of 1990, when vandals set it on fire and burned the northern half almost beyond repair. An organized effort by local citizens and historical officials was successful in raising enough funds for the complete restoration of the bridge. It was rebuilt by the Limberlost Construction Company and reopened to public traffic in July 1992, even though it was already bypassed with a new concrete bridge in 1983. The Roann Bridge is the fourth covered bridge at this site; the first was built in 1841. Today, it is protected with a modern fire sprinkler system and serves as a model for other covered bridge preservation projects. The Roann Bridge was listed on the National Register of Historic Places in August 1991.

1884, W.G. No. 15-61-04
MADISON COUNTY, IOWA
PHOTO BY THOMAS E. WALCZAK

HOGBACK BRIDGE

One of six remaining covered bridges in Madison County, the Hogback Bridge dates back to 1884 when it was first constructed by Benton Jones over the North River on Douglas Township Road. It is built with the Town lattice truss system and has a length of 106 feet. The unusual flat roof was used on several Iowa covered bridges and at least one in Ohio. Hogback Bridge sits on steel pylons and has a long approach ramp at each end. In 1992, it was renovated at a cost of $188,810.

ROSEMAN/OAK GROVE BRIDGE

Perhaps the most famous covered bridge in the world, due to its staring role in the popular novel The Bridges of Madison County, the Roseman Bridge has brought thousands of new visitors to Madison County, Iowa, in the past couple of years. It was constructed 113 years ago using the Town and queen trusses and sits on steel pylons with long approach ramps leading to each end. The unusual flat roof sets it apart from most other covered bridges, with the exception of three in the same county. Roseman Bridge spans the Middle River and measures 106 feet in length. No longer used for automobile traffic, it is still kept in excellent condition.

TOWN

TRUSS

1883, W.G. No. 15-61-07
MADISON COUNTY, IOWA
PHOTO BY SHIMA YOSHIO

HOWE
TRUSS

1870, W.G. No. 15-63-01
MARION COUNTY, IOWA
PHOTO BY SHIMA YOSHIO

HAMMOND BRIDGE

The Hammond Bridge is one of only three covered bridges still open to automobile traffic in the state of Iowa. Originally constructed in 1870 with the Howe truss system, it spans the North Cedar Creek with a length of 80 feet. Red vertical siding protects the trusses, and a large horizontal vent runs the length of the structure just under the roof overhang. There is an open approach ramp on each end of the bridge, and height barriers to keep large vehicles from using the old bridge. It is located south of Attica on Indiana Township Road.

SWITZER BRIDGE

One of 15 remaining covered bridges in Kentucky, the Switzer Bridge is in excellent condition thanks to a major restoration in 1991-1992. It was built by George Hockensmith using the Howe truss system and sits on dry laid stone abutments, one of which is reinforced with concrete. It crosses the North Elkhorn Creek with a length of 120 feet and is 11 feet wide. Closed and bypassed in 1954, it is now a memorial to the old ways of transportation in the nineteenth century. A park area surrounds the bridge, where visitors can enjoy the quiet scene while having a picnic. In 1974, the bridge was placed on the National Register of Historic Places. Switzer Bridge can be located by going 4 miles east of Frankfort on US460, then north 3.6 miles on KY1262; the bridge is on the right side, just before the town of Switzer.

HOWE
TRUSS

1855, W.G. No. 17-37-01
FRANKLIN COUNTY, KENTUCKY
PHOTO BY BRIAN J. McKEE

BENNETT MILL BRIDGE

Bennett Mill Bridge is certainly one of the most interesting examples of covered bridge design in the country, being the only remaining Wheeler truss bridge. This unusual truss was patented in 1870 by Isaac H. Wheeler of Portsmouth, Ohio, and is mainly distinguished by its additional chord, which runs horizontally, halfway between the upper and lower chords. Crossing the Tygart's Creek, it measures 158 feet, 10 inches long and sits on cut stone abutments, which were taken from the old Globe Furnace, once located near the end of the bridge. It is the longest single-span covered bridge in the state, and is in very good condition considering that it is used daily for automobile traffic, a stress that it was never designed for. There is a small amount of steel reinforcement under the bridge along the lower chords; however, the structure is basically unchanged since it was built 141 years ago by B.F. and Pramley Bennett. The Bennetts operated a mill along Tygart's Creek at the time. Bennett Mill Bridge is located 8.5 miles south of South Shore, Kentucky, on KY7, then just east on KY1215
(Tygart's Creek Road).

1855, W.G. No. 17-45-01
GREENUP COUNTY, KENTUCKY
PHOTO BY BRIAN J. McKEE

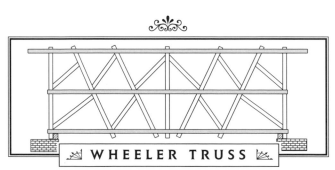

WHEELER TRUSS

The picturesque Hemlock Bridge uses the Paddleford truss reinforced with an arch to span the Old Channel of the Saco River. It was built in 1857 and measures 116 feet in length. Visitors can find it on Hemlock Bridge Road northwest of East Fryeburg.

HEMLOCK BRIDGE

1857, W.G. No. 19-09-02
OXFORD COUNTY, MAINE
PHOTO BY SHIMA YOSHIO

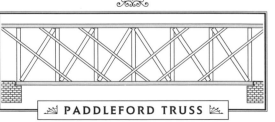

PADDLEFORD TRUSS

SUNDAY RIVER BRIDGE

The scenic Sunday River Bridge is sometimes called the "Artist Bridge." It spans the Sunday River on Sunday River Road northwest of North Bethel. The siding leaves the upper half of the trusses exposed, and the roof has a long overhang to keep the rain out. The 100 foot long Paddleford truss was built in 1870, but is no longer used as it has been bypassed with a modern bridge.

PADDLEFORD

TRUSS

1870, W.G. No. 19-09-04
OXFORD COUNTY, MAINE
PHOTO BY SHIMA YOSHIO

43

The Porter/Parsonfield Bridge joins the counties of Oxford and York by crossing the Ossippee River. The name comes from the two townships that it resides in. Its 160 foot Paddleford truss uses two spans and has large laminated arches on each span. It sits on cut stone abutments and a center pier. The floor is interesting in that it is made of rectangular blocks of asphalt. Located south of Porter on ME160, it has been bypassed with a more modern bridge and no longer carries traffic.

PORTER/ PARSONFIELD BRIDGE

1858, W.G. No. 19-09-05/16-01
OXFORD/YORK COUNTIES, MAINE
PHOTO BY SHIMA YOSHIO

PADDLEFORD
TRUSS

Jericho Bridge

The Jericho Bridge spans the Little Gunpowder Falls Creek on Jericho Road ENE of Kingsville, Maryland, joining Baltimore and Harford Counties. It was built by Thomas F. Forsyth in 1858 with a combination of three different types of trusses: queen post, multiple king post, and arch. It has a total length of 88 feet. This has been a bridge of many colors over the years: red, white, green, and presently brown. It received major repairs in 1981 and is currently open to traffic.

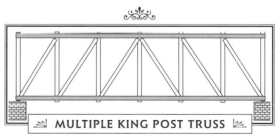

MULTIPLE KING POST TRUSS

1858, W.G. No. 20-03-02/12-01
Baltimore and Harford Counties, Maryland
Photo by Joanne Schmitz

GILPIN'S BRIDGE

1860, W.G. No. 20-07-01
CECIL COUNTY, MARYLAND
PHOTO BY JOANNE SCHMITZ

Gilpin's Bridge crosses the North East Creek in the town of Bayview, in Cecil County, Maryland. This 119 foot long single-span bridge was built in 1860 with the Burr arch truss system. The arches are unusual in that they are each made from two separate pieces of timber. There once was a flour mill nearby owned by Samuel Gilpins. It can be easily seen alongside Route 272, where it was bypassed several years ago.

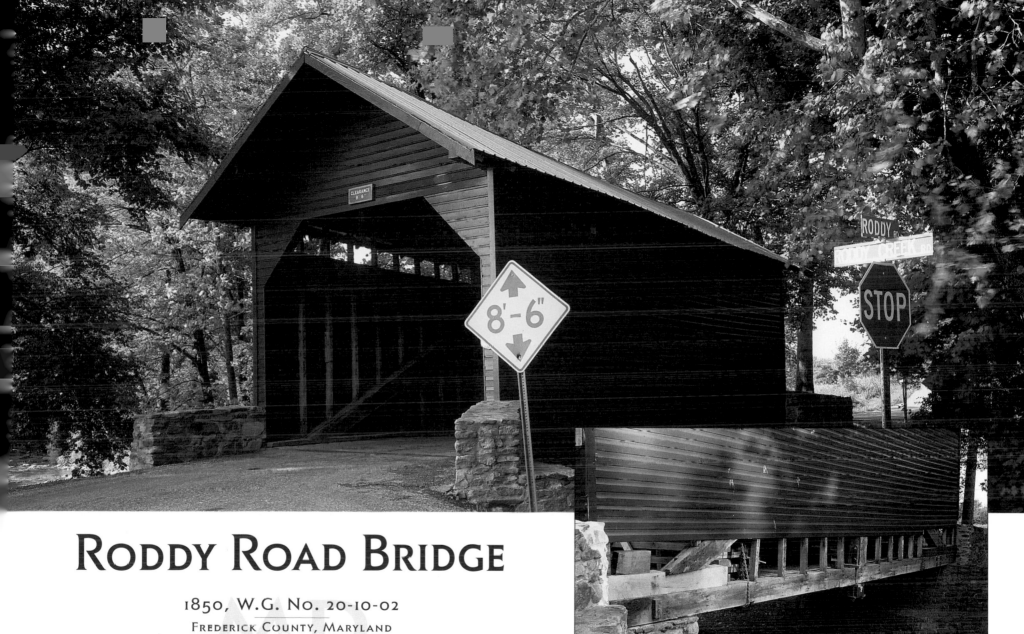

RODDY ROAD BRIDGE

1850, W.G. No. 20-10-02
FREDERICK COUNTY, MARYLAND
PHOTO BY BRIAN J. McKEE

The Roddy Road Bridge is Maryland's shortest covered bridge at 39 feet, and is one of three that remain in Frederick County. It crosses the Owens Creek with a single-span king-post truss and sits on beautiful stone and mortar abutments. The bridge is painted dark red and has a metal roof. Restored in 1995 by Dean Fitzgerald, it is kept in excellent condition and remains open to automobile traffic. It is located a mile north of Thurmont and a mile east of US15 on Roddy Road.

KING TRUSS

BURKVILLE BRIDGE

HOWE TRUSS

1870, W.G. No. 21-06-01
FRANKLIN COUNTY, MASSACHUSETTS
PHOTO BY RICHARD T. DONOVAN

The Burkville Bridge is representative of a typical nineteenth-century Massachusetts covered bridge. It is no longer open to traffic, but is preserved as a historical relic of the past. Measuring 106 feet in length, it sits high above the South River with an unusual single-span Howe truss system. Its truss panels have only one wooden element instead of two as in most Howe trusses. Only the Bean Blossom Bridge in Indiana has a similar design. Its naturally aged vertical siding has turned a variety of colors over the years. A full-length vent runs along each side just under the roof line, and on one side there are several open windows for light and ventilation. Concrete abutments support each end of the bridge. Burkville Bridge is located in the town of Conway, just south of MA116 on Poland Road.

FALLASBURG BRIDGE

The Fallasburg Bridge is one of only two remaining Brown truss covered bridges in the country and is the oldest one by 25 years. The other example of the Brown truss is the White Bridge in Ionia County, Michigan, southwest of Belding. Fallasburg Bridge was built over the Flat River in Vergennes Township with a single span and is still open to traffic. It measures 100 feet in length and sits on concrete abutments. There is a park next to it that allows visitors a great side view of this historic structure. It is located north of Lowell on Lincoln Lake Road, then east on Fallasburg Park Road to Covered Bridge Road.

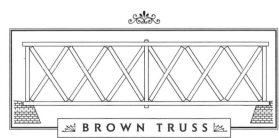

≥ BROWN TRUSS ≤

1871, W.G. No. 22-41-02
KENT COUNTY, MICHIGAN
PHOTO BY BRIAN J. McKEE

ZUMBROTA BRIDGE

TOWN
TRUSS

1869, W.G. No. 23-25-01
GOODHUE COUNTY, MINNESOTA
PHOTO BY SHIMA YOSHIO

Minnesota's last remaining covered bridge is no longer asked to carry public transportation along the old stagecoach route from Dubuque to St. Paul, but fortunately has been well preserved by the local citizens. It was originally built in 1869 over the Zumbro River, not far from its present location, and uses a Town lattice truss system that measures 120 feet in length. In 1932 it was moved to the fairgrounds where it rested until 1970, when it was moved to Covered Bridge Park.

BOLLINGER MILL BRIDGE

The Bollinger Mill Bridge is one of the few covered bridge and mill combinations remaining in the country and offers visitors a wonderful view of the way of life in the nineteenth century. Since a mill was the center of activity in the community, it was practical to build a bridge nearby to accommodate the mill's customers. Built in 1868, the bridge uses a single-span Howe truss 140 feet in length to bring its travelers across the Whitewater River. It is located southwest of Jackson at Burfordville on county road HH.

HOWE TRUSS

1868, W.G. No. 25-16-01
CAPE GIRARDEAU COUNTY, MISSOURI
PHOTO BY SHIMA YOSHIO

Although closed to automobile traffic, the Union Bridge still proves useful to some travelers who need to cross the Elk Fork of the Salt River. It was built in 1871 using the Burr truss system and measures 125 feet in length. Visitors can locate it southwest of Paris on a road off county road CC.

UNION BRIDGE

1871, W.G. No. 25-69-02
MONROE COUNTY, MISSOURI
PHOTO BY SHIMA YOSHIO

BURR
TRUSS

SACO RIVER BRIDGE

Using a two-span Paddleford truss system with wooden arches, the Saco River Bridge still carries traffic across the Saco River at Conway, as it has for the past 106 years. It is in such immaculate condition that it gives visitors the impression that it was just recently built. In fact, between 1987 and 1989, it was extensively restored by the New Hampshire Department of Transportation, probably at a much greater expense than its original cost of $4000. It measures 224 feet in length and is supported by two stone abutments and a stone center pier. Built by Charles and Frank Broughton, it is the third wooden bridge to be located at this site since 1850.

PADDLEFORD

TRUSS

1890, W.G. No. 29-02-03
CARROLL COUNTY, NEW HAMPSHIRE
PHOTO BY BRIAN J. McKEE

UPPER VILLAGE/ASHUELOT BRIDGE

The Upper Village or Ashuelot Bridge is known as a "village" style bridge because of its dual sidewalks, which are covered by the same roof as the main roadway bridge. They are a congruent part of the whole structure, not tacked-on additions. It has carried both pedestrian and vehicular traffic safely across the Ashuelot River for the past 132 years. There is no siding on the bridge, but it is well protected by a heavy coating of white paint inside and out, giving it a bright, airy atmosphere. It uses a two-span Town lattice truss system that measures 169 feet in length and has a single pier in the center for added support. With its ornate portal designs trimmed in red, this romantic structure is the subject of many artists and photographers and is listed on the National Register of Historic Places. It is located just south of NH119 in Winchester on Bolton Road.

TOWN TRUSS

1864, W.G. No. 29-03-02
CHESHIRE COUNTY, NEW HAMPSHIRE
PHOTO BY BRIAN J. McKEE

BATH BRIDGE

BURR

TRUSS

1832, W.G. No. 29-05-03

GRAFTON COUNTY, NEW HAMPSHIRE

PHOTO BY BRIAN J. McKEE

The Bath Bridge is a rare combination of extreme length and very old age. Most wooden covered bridges of such length have not survived in this age of heavy loads and fast-moving automobile traffic. Measuring 375 feet long, the rustic Bath Bridge still carries its travelers over the Ammonoosuc River and the Boston & Maine Railroad line. It uses four spans and is built with a Burr truss system. Situated in the quiet village of Bath, it preserves a rapidly vanishing scene from the American nineteenth century.

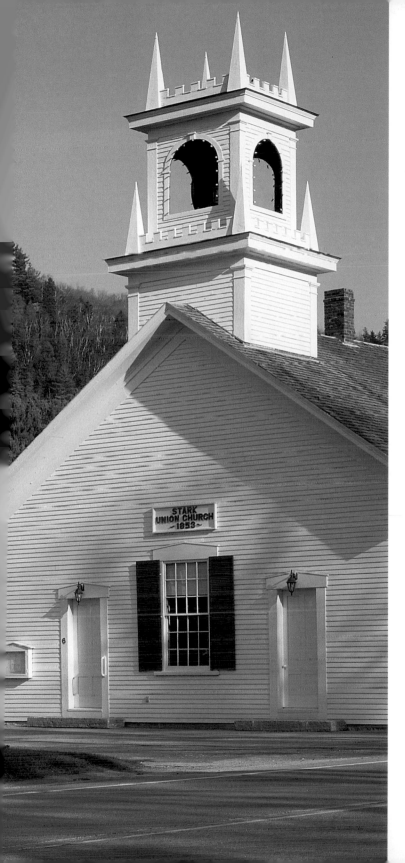

STARK BRIDGE

With the Long Mountains in the background and the little white Union Church at its side, the Stark Covered Bridge provides us with one of the most picturesque scenes in America. This beautiful setting, along with the ornate treatment of the portals, attracts bridge enthusiasts and artists from all over the world. Its dual sidewalks are an integral part of the whole structure, which is covered by one main roof, making it a true "village style" bridge. It uses the Paddleford truss system to span the Upper Ammonoosuc River and measures 134 feet long. Restored several times during its lengthy existence, it now has steel stringer beams and a concrete center pier under it for increased load capacity. Several residents have placed their mailboxes inside it, to keep them protected from the weather. It is located just off NH110 at the village of Stark, and is listed on the National Register of Historic Places.

1862, W.G. No. 29-04-05
Coos County, New Hampshire
Photo by Brian J. McKee

PADDLEFORD
TRUSS

BATH/HAVERHILL BRIDGE

Although situated in the village of Woodsville on NH135, the bridge carries traffic between the towns of Bath and Haverhill, and was so named in its early days. It crosses the Ammonoosuc River with a two-span Town lattice truss system with an arch, and measures 277 feet in length. A sidewalk is attached to one side for safer pedestrian travel. Still open to automobile traffic, it has been well maintained over the past 167 years. It is the oldest covered bridge in use in the state of New Hampshire and perhaps in the entire country.

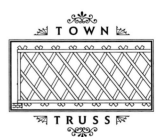

TOWN TRUSS

1829, W.G. NO. 29-05-04
GRAFTON COUNTY, NEW HAMPSHIRE
PHOTO BY BRIAN J. MCKEE

BLAIR BRIDGE

1869, W.G. No. 29-05-09
GRAFTON COUNTY, NEW HAMPSHIRE
PHOTO BY BRIAN J. MCKEE

At 293 feet in length, the Blair Bridge is another of Grafton County's extremely long covered bridges. Remarkably, it still carries automobile traffic across the Pemigewasset River with two spans using the Long truss system and arch. The dry laid stone abutments and center pier are interesting in themselves. It is located northeast of Plymouth on Blair Road, about 2 miles north of Livermore Falls.

LONG TRUSS

SULPHITE RAILROAD BRIDGE

The Sulphite Railroad Bridge is unique in the fact that it carried trains over the roof instead of through the interior. Originally built by the Boston & Maine Railroad, it is the only surviving deck-type covered bridge in America. The bridge was nearly lost, though, when arsonists set it on fire in October of 1980, and burned all the siding off. It was closed to traffic in 1973, and has remained as a popular local historic attraction ever since. It uses the Pratt truss system to cross the Winnipesaukee River in three spans and measures 180 feet long. The approaches add another 51 feet to this length. Located about a quarter mile down the old railroad grade from the town of Franklin, it sits quietly while local preservation efforts gather the funds to restore it.

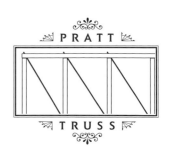

PRATT TRUSS

1896, W.G. No. 29-07-09
MERRIMACK COUNTY, NEW HAMPSHIRE
PHOTO BY BRIAN J. MCKEE

PIER RAILROAD BRIDGE

1907, W.G. No. 29-10-03
SULLIVAN COUNTY, NEW HAMPSHIRE
PHOTO BY BRIAN J. McKEE

The rare Pier Railroad Bridge serves as an outstanding example of what was once a commonplace type of covered bridge in the United States. Today, there are no railroad covered bridges being used for actual rail traffic, although one is used for an amusement ride. The Pier Bridge crosses the Sugar River with two spans and uses a combination double Pratt and Town truss system that measures 228 feet in length. It was built by the Boston & Maine Railroad to replace an earlier wooden bridge. Located west of Kelleyville on the north side of Chandler Road, the bridge is now part of a bike trail. Another railroad covered bridge, the Wright Bridge, exists just 1 mile away on the same line.

TOWN

TRUSS

GREEN SERGEANTS BRIDGE

Green Sergeants Bridge is the sole survivor of covered bridges in the state of New Jersey. Local enthusiasm for the bridge has kept it from being removed, and it still serves the public by carrying traffic over the Wickeheoke Creek, even though it was bypassed with a more modern bridge several years ago. The arrangement is unique in that the covered bridge carries traffic in one direction, while the modern bridge carries traffic going the opposite direction. Built with an 84 foot long queen-post truss in 1866, the bridge has been reinforced with steel members to increase its load capacity. It is located on CR604, west of Sergeantsville.

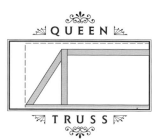

QUEEN

TRUSS

1866, W.G. No. 30-10-01
HUNTERDON COUNTY, NEW JERSEY
PHOTO BY BRIAN J. McKEE

The signs on the bridge read:

NO LOITERING OR STANDING BY ORDER TOWN OF COLCHESTER

6 FT. 0 IN CLEARANCE

WEIGHT LIMIT 3 TONS

ONE VEHICLE ON BRIDGE AT A TIME

WELCOME TO DOWNSVILLE SETTLED IN 1792

LONG TRUSS

1854, W.G. NO. 32-13-01
DELAWARE COUNTY, NEW YORK
PHOTO BY RICHARD WILSON

DOWNSVILLE BRIDGE

The Downsville Bridge was built by Robert Murray for $1700 and has the distinction of being New York's second-longest covered span. It has a very rustic quality due to the old weathered siding, which has likely not ever been painted. Made from a combination of both Long and queen-post trusses, it crosses the East Branch of the Delaware river with a single span and measures 174 feet in length. The bridge had served public faithfully for 141 years until it was closed to automobile traffic in 1994 for safety reasons. It is located on the south edge of Downsville in Colchester Township, just west of the Pepacton Reservoir.

FITCHES BRIDGE

Fitches Bridge was originally built in 1870 on Kingston Street in Delhi, New York, by James Frazier and James Warren. In 1885, it was dismantled by David L. Wright and re-erected 3 miles upstream, still across the West Branch of the Delaware River. When it was relocated, it was turned end for end, and now faces the opposite direction that it did originally. It uses a 100 foot Town truss system for its support and has flying buttresses on the sides to keep it from leaning. The bridge is easy to find just off NY10 about 3.5 miles north of Delhi at East Delhi.

TOWN TRUSS

1870, W.G. No. 32-13-02
DELAWARE COUNTY, NEW YORK
PHOTO BY RICHARD WILSON

The Buskirk Bridge joins Rensselaer County and Washington County together by crossing the Hoosic River at the town of Buskirk. It uses a single-span Howe truss that measures 164 feet long, and as of this writing, is posted with a 6 ton weight limit. This photogenic bridge is painted bright red with white trim, and has a total of 12 windows to allow air and light inside. The present bridge replaced at least two earlier bridges at the same crossing, and was built by Osterhauth & Newman of Waterford, New York, for about $1500. It is located at Buskirk on NY103/59. This road was once part of the Great Northern Turnpike, which was constructed in 1799.

BUSKIRK BRIDGE

1857, W.G. No. 32-42-02/58-04
RENSSELAER/WASHINGTON COUNTIES, NEW YORK
PHOTO BY RICHARD WILSON

HOWE TRUSS

BUSKIRKS BRIDGE
25 Dollars Fine for Driving on this Bridge Faster than a Walk.

10'-0"
CLEARANCE

WEIGHT
LIMIT
6
TONS

BLENHEIM BRIDGE

LONG TRUSS

1855, W.G. No. 32-48-01
SCHOHARIE COUNTY, NEW YORK
PHOTO BY RICHARD WILSON

The Blenheim Bridge is quite an interesting structure as it is the world's longest remaining single-span covered bridge at 232 feet, and is also a true double-barreled bridge, with a complete truss network running down its center as well as each side. It uses the Long truss system with massive arches for more support. Designated a National Civil Engineering Landmark in 1984, the Blenheim Bridge is one of only three covered bridges to receive this honor. The others are California's Bridgeport Bridge and the Cornish-Windsor Bridge, which connects Vermont with New Hampshire. Now retired from public service, it has been bypassed since 1931 with a modern iron bridge. It was originally built in 1855 by Nicholas M. Powers over the Schoharie Creek. An iron span was added to west end in 1869 when the riverbank was washed out by flood waters. The iron span was removed several years ago. It is easy to locate as it rests along the side of NY30 at North Blenheim.

The sign on the bridge reads: $500 FINE TO RIDE OR DRIVE THIS BRIDGE FASTER THAN A WALK

NEWFIELD BRIDGE

The third-oldest covered bridge remaining in the state of New York was built 143 years ago in the town of Newfield over the West Branch of the Cayuga Creek. It crosses the creek by using a single-span Town lattice truss system and measures 115 feet in length. In 1972, it was rebuilt by the Graton & Associates of Ashland, New Hampshire, and is in excellent condition today, still open to the public. It is located on Bridge Street between Main and Bank Streets.

TOWN TRUSS

1853, W.G. No. 32-55-01
TOMPKINS COUNTY, NEW YORK
PHOTO BY RICHARD WILSON

Grant's Mills Bridge

☆ T O W N ☆

☆ T R U S S ☆

1902, W.G. No. 32-56-06
ULSTER COUNTY, NEW YORK
PHOTO BY BRIAN J. MCKEE

The Grant's Mills Bridge was built 94 years ago by Edgar Marks, Orrin B. Marks, Wesley Alton, and Myron Hall for $1027.97. It spans 66 feet over the Mill Brook in Hardenbergh Township. It uses the Town lattice truss system with wooden trunnels holding all the wooden members together. The bridge's distinctive appearance comes from the eight flying buttresses that keep it from twisting or leaning. It has been closed and bypassed, but is in excellent condition today, thanks to the efforts of Bob Vredenburgh. A direct descendent of the original builders, Bob Vredenburgh undertook the monumental task of restoring the bridge to pristine condition in October 1990. Twenty months and over $13,000 later, the restoration was completed. The bridge is located along Mill Brook Road, south of Margaretville.

REXLEIGH BRIDGE

The Rexleigh Bridge is one of four existing old covered bridges in Washington County and is an outstanding example of a Howe truss system. It measures 107 feet in length and crosses the Batten Kill River with a single span, resting on stone abutments. One of the abutments contains several granite blocks that are in sharp contrast to the other type of stone used in it. The bridge was restored in 1984 and remains open to traffic. It is located on the Jackson/Salem Township line, about 2 miles south of Salem on NY29, then left on Rexleigh Road for another 1.5 miles.

HOWE
TRUSS

1874, W.G. No. 32-58-03
WASHINGTON COUNTY, NEW YORK
PHOTO BY RICHARD WILSON

BUNKER HILL BRIDGE

The Bunker Hill Bridge is North Carolina's only true wooden truss covered bridge, and also has the distinction of being only one of two remaining Haupt trusses left in the country. It spans Lyle Creek with a length of 85 feet and is located east of Claremont near a roadside park off old Route 64/70. It was completely restored in 1994 and is closed to automobile traffic.

HAUPT
TRUSS

1894, W.G. No. 33-18-01
CATAWBA COUNTY, NORTH CAROLINA
PHOTO BY SHIMA YOSHIO

HARPERSFIELD BRIDGE

1868, W.G. No. 35-04-19
ASHTABULA COUNTY, OHIO
PHOTO BY BRIAN J. MCKEE

HOWE TRUSS

Measuring 234 feet in length, the Harpersfield Bridge has the distinction of being Ohio's longest covered bridge. After the flood of 1913 caused the widening of the river at the bridge site, a 140 foot steel span was added to the end of the covered bridge, making a combined total length of 374 feet. The wooden bridge uses two Howe truss spans to cross the Grand River, and has five additional steel piers under it for extra support. In 1992, a complete renovation of the bridge was done by the Ashtabula County engineer, John Smolen, and a much needed exterior sidewalk was added for pedestrians, drastically changing the appearance of the old landmark. It was bypassed with a newer concrete bridge upstream, but still seems to carry an enormous amount of traffic on CR154. It was originally on OH534, until the bypass bridge was built. The scenic location of the Harpersfield Bridge, with a roaring dam in the background, attracts many fishermen, artists, and photographers from around the world.

71

The Warner Hollow Bridge, or Wiswell Road Bridge, as it is sometimes referred to, crosses the Phelps Creek in dramatic style. It sits high above a scenic gorge resting on two massive stone piers that must be 50 feet above the riverbed. Both the 120 foot long bridge and the road have been closed for many years, and the area is now used for hiking. The bridge was built with the Town lattice truss system, as were many of the Ashtabula County covered bridges. One of 15 existing covered wooden spans in the county, it has fallen into poor condition in recent years, however it is scheduled to be renovated in the near future. Visitors can find it located in the southwest corner of Ashtabula County, in Windsor Township, just south of US322 on Wiswell Road (TR357).

WARNER HOLLOW BRIDGE

1867, W.G. No. 35-04-25
ASHTABULA COUNTY, OHIO
PHOTO BY BRIAN J. McKEE

TOWN

TRUSS

BOWMAN/EAGLE CREEK BRIDGE

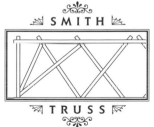

SMITH TRUSS

1875, W.G. No. 35-08-18
BROWN COUNTY, OHIO
PHOTO BY BRIAN J. McKEE

At 186.5 feet in length, the Eagle Creek, or Bowman, Bridge is Ohio's longest remaining single-span covered bridge. This is a remarkable length for a wooden bridge considering that it is used daily by automobile traffic and has absolutely no additional means of support or reinforcement. It uses the Smith truss system to cross the Eagle Creek and is the only covered bridge on an Ohio state highway. Despite vandalism and traffic accidents, the bridge looks to be in almost new condition, with not a bit of negative camber in its trusses. One of five covered bridges in Brown County, it is the only one that is painted. It is located in a quiet valley on OH763, about 4.5 miles south of OH125.

The Bebb Park or State Line Bridge is unique in that it is the only remaining Wernwag truss covered bridge in the world. It was moved from its original location on Fairfield Road in 1966 to the Governor Bebb Historical Park in this western Ohio county and spans a dry ravine. It measures 120 feet long and sits along the east side of the main entrance road to the park, which is a Morgan Township road going south off of OH126.

BEBB PARK BRIDGE

c1873, W.G. No. 35-09-02
BUTLER COUNTY, OHIO
PHOTO BY BRIAN J. McKEE

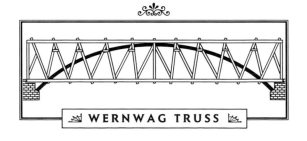

WERNWAG TRUSS

The last covered bridge in Clermont County was named for the nearby town of Perintown. Built 118 years ago, it still carries traffic across the Stonelick Creek with its 140 foot Howe truss structure. With its bright red paint, the old bridge appears to be in excellent shape, despite being damaged several times over the years by overweight trucks. It is located on CR116 in Stonelick Township, about a mile north of US50.

PERINTOWN/ STONELICK BRIDGE

1878, W.G. No. 35-13-02
CLERMONT COUNTY, OHIO
PHOTO BY BRIAN J. MCKEE

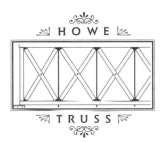

HOWE

TRUSS

The rustic Lynchburg Bridge joins the counties of Clinton and Highland by crossing the East Fork of the Miami River with a single span. It was built by John Gregg for $3138 and uses a Long truss system with a length of 117 feet. The bridge has been closed to traffic since 1969, although it appears to be in very sturdy condition. In the winter of 1993, it was burned by arsonists and the roof was badly damaged. For two years, it sat untouched until the fall of 1995, when it was finally repaired. The Lynchburg Bridge is located on High Street on the west side of the town of Lynchburg in Clark Township (Dodson Township in Highland County).

LYNCHBURG BRIDGE

1870, W.G. No. 35-14-11 OR 36-06
CLINTON AND HIGHLAND COUNTIES OHIO
PHOTO BY BRIAN J. McKEE

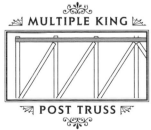

MULTIPLE KING

POST TRUSS

1871, W.G. No. 35-15-02
COLUMBIANA COUNTY, OHIO
PHOTO BY BRIAN J. MCKEE

MCCLELLAN BRIDGE

The McClellan Bridge is intriguing for the fact that it sits down in a hidden valley on an old abandoned dirt road and appears to be long forgotten. Built 125 years ago, it uses a simple multiple king-post truss to span the West Fork of the Little Beaver Creek in Center Township. It rests on TR871, which is no longer open to the public, but is apparently only used for farm vehicles. The 53 foot long bridge is in good condition for being abandoned, and its unpainted natural wood siding has become a colorful array of vertical boards due to their occasional, random replacement. It is located southwest of Lisbon just off the east side of Little Trinity Church Road (TR756).

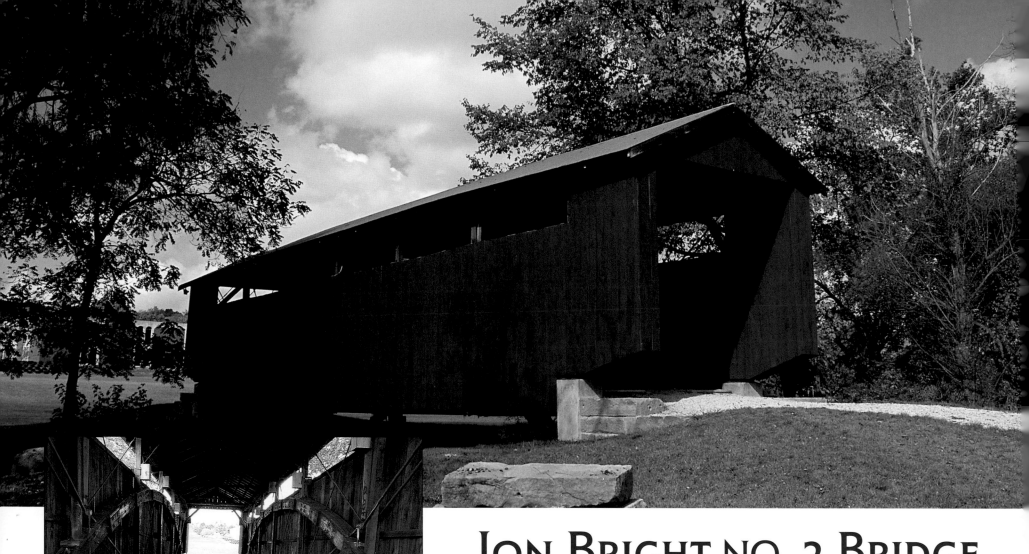

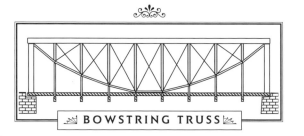

JON BRIGHT NO. 2 BRIDGE

1881, W.G. No. 35-23-10
FAIRFIELD COUNTY, OHIO
PHOTO BY BRIAN J. MCKEE

BOWSTRING TRUSS

The Jon Bright No. 2 Bridge is unique in the fact that it uses a combination of an inverted iron bowstring truss and a wooden arch for support. It was designed and built by August Borneman, a well-known local bridge contractor. Named for a nearby landowner in Pleasant Township, the 75 foot bridge originally crossed the Poplar Creek on TR263. In 1988, it was moved by Ohio University and now spans Fetter's Run where it has been completely restored and is well maintained. Jon Bright No. 2 Bridge is listed on the National Register of Historic Places. Today, it is located at the rear of the Ohio University campus just north of Lancaster on the east side of OH37.

Mink Hollow Bridge

The charming, peaceful setting of this little white Fairfield County covered bridge is a favorite of many artists, photographers, and bridge enthusiasts. It is typical of the style of the hundreds of covered bridges that were constructed in this southern Ohio county during the nineteenth century. Today, it is one of only 15 old wooden spans that still exist in a community that once boasted of having the highest number of them in the state. The Mink Hollow Bridge is a single-span multiple king-post truss structure and measures 51 feet in length. It crosses the Arney Run with a noticeable positive camber, an indication that it is still in excellent condition. Its full-length shaded windows and bright tin roof add to its romantic appearance and provide protection from the weather while allowing ventilation and light to enter. It was closed and bypassed in 1992, but is watched closely by neighbors who have a great appreciation of their old historical landmark. A small park has been created next to the bridge, a great place for a picnic. Visitors can find the Mink Hollow Bridge by taking Hamburg Road south from Lancaster to Hopewell Church Road, turn left and go to Meister Road, then just right on Crooks Road.

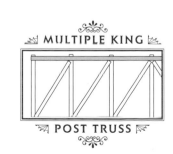

MULTIPLE KING

POST TRUSS

1887, W.G. No. 35-23-43
FAIRFIELD COUNTY, OHIO
PHOTO BY BRIAN J. McKEE

BERGSTRESSER/DIETZ/ASHBROOK ROAD BRIDGE

1887 W.G. No. 35-25-03
FRANKLIN COUNTY, OHIO
PHOTO BY BRIAN J. MCKEE

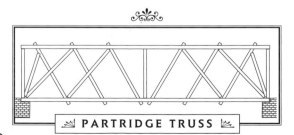

PARTRIDGE TRUSS

A sign on the portal states that this is "The Last Covered Bridge in Franklin County," and it is obvious that the local residents are doing a wonderful job of keeping it in excellent condition for future generations to enjoy. Built in 1887 using the rare Partridge truss design, it crosses the Little Walnut Creek with a length of 134 feet. It is the only remaining example of the Partridge truss outside Union County, Ohio, and is also the longest since the loss of the Reed Bridge in Union County a couple of years ago. It is closed to traffic, but can be located just south of Canal Winchester on OH674, then west at Ashbrook Road.

BALLARD ROAD BRIDGE

The Ballard Road Bridge is one of five covered bridges still standing in Greene County, and one of three still open to traffic. It crosses the north branch of Caesars Creek with an 80 foot single-span Howe truss, and uses a small amount of steel reinforcement on its lower chords. The bridge and stonework were built by J.C. Brown and Henry E. Hebble. It is located halfway between Xenia and Jamestown on US35, then a half mile south on Ballard Road.

1883, W.G. No. 35-29-18
Greene County, Ohio
Photo by Brian J. McKee

HOWE

TRUSS

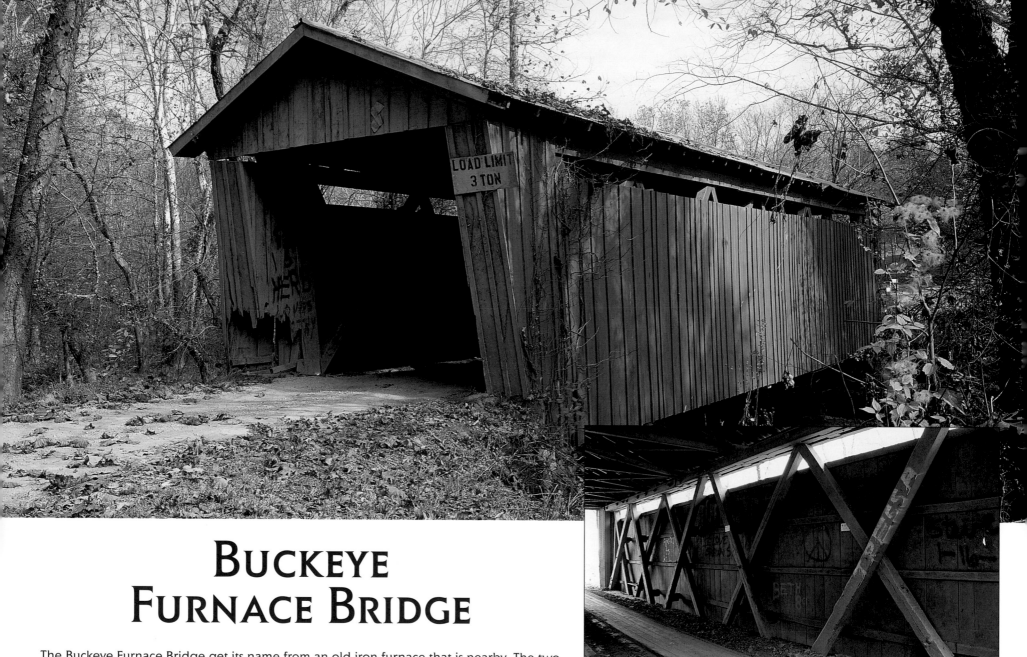

BUCKEYE FURNACE BRIDGE

The Buckeye Furnace Bridge get its name from an old iron furnace that is nearby. The two historic structures together make a very interesting combination, and visitors can also tour the original company store, which has been turned into a museum by the Ohio Historical Society. The bridge was built over the Little Raccoon Creek by Dency, McCurdy, & Co. with a 59 foot Smith truss and is still open to automobile traffic. It is located southeast of Wellston. Take OH124 east to the Buckeye Furnace Road (CR58), turn right, then go to TR165 and turn right to the furnace. The bridge is straight ahead, just past the furnace.

1871, W.G. No. 35-40-11
JACKSON COUNTY, OHIO
PHOTO BY BRIAN J. MCKEE

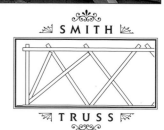

SMITH
TRUSS

One of seven wooden truss covered bridges in Licking County, the Boy Scout Bridge was moved to its present location in 1974 in order to preserve it. It originally was located about a mile away on Rocky Fork Road over the Rainrock Creek. It uses a 49 foot single-span multiple king-post truss and sits over the Rocky Fork Creek inside a Boy Scout camp. Now used only for storage, it rests in an quiet, attractive setting and is kept in excellent condition. It is located northeast of Newark in Eden Township off the west side of Rocky Fork Road (CR210). Visitors must park inside the scout camp, then walk a quarter mile southwest around a pond to get the bridge.

BOY SCOUT BRIDGE

DATE UNKNOWN, W.G. NO. 35-45-04
LICKING COUNTY, OHIO
PHOTO BY BRIAN J. MCKEE

MULTIPLE KING

POST TRUSS

⚓ L O N G ⚓
T R U S S

1860, W.G. No. 35-55-01
MIAMI COUNTY, OHIO
PHOTO BY BRIAN J. McKEE

ELDEAN BRIDGE

The Eldean Bridge is named for the small town of Eldean nearby. It crosses the Great Miami River with a two-span Long truss system and measures 228 feet in length, making it Ohio's second-longest covered bridge. Built by James and William Hamilton at a cost of $11.75 per linear foot, the bridge is very well maintained and is still open to traffic despite being bypassed with a new concrete bridge in 1964. It is located about 2 miles north of Troy on CR25, then east on CR33 (Eldean Road) at a park.

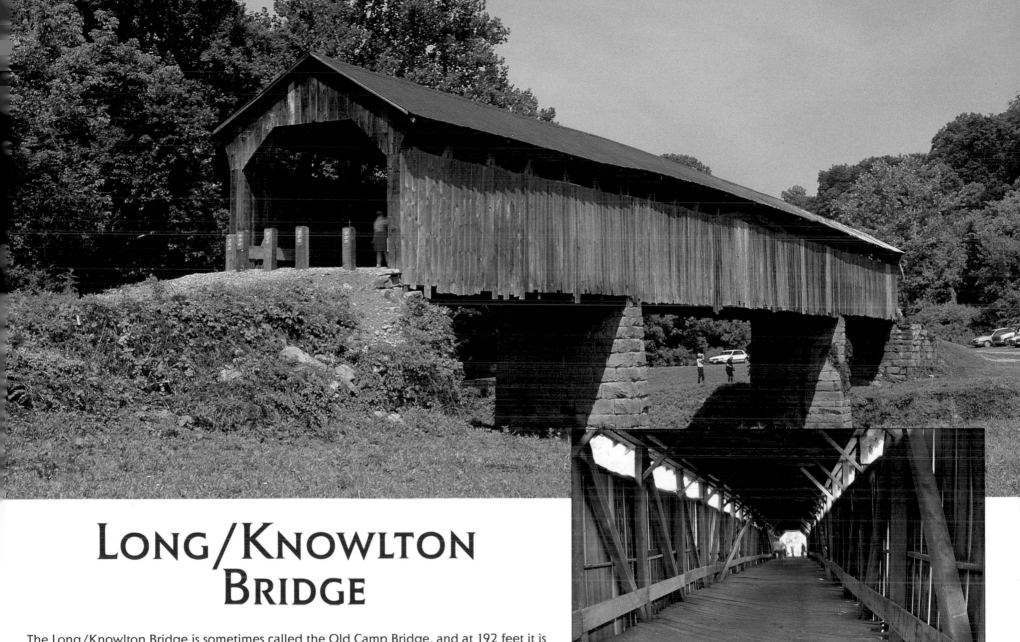

LONG/KNOWLTON BRIDGE

The Long/Knowlton Bridge is sometimes called the Old Camp Bridge, and at 192 feet it is the fourth-longest covered bridge in the state. It sits high above the Little Muskingum River by using a three-span multiple king-post truss system and an arch in the center section. The huge cut stone abutments and center piers are fascinating and serve to prevent the bridge from being washed away in a flood. There is a park on its north side, where visitors can relax and enjoy the beautiful southern Ohio scenery with the bridge in the foreground. It was restored in July of 1995, but kept closed to traffic. The location is in Washington Township, north of Rinard Mills on OH26, then a quarter mile east on TR38.

1887, W.G. No. 35-56-18
MONROE COUNTY, OHIO
PHOTO BY BRIAN J. MCKEE

⚜ MULTIPLE KING ⚜

POST TRUSS

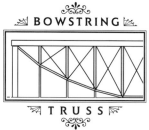

BOWSTRING TRUSS

1865, W.G. No. 35-57-01
MONTGOMERY COUNTY, OHIO
PHOTO BY BRIAN J. MCKEE

GERMANTOWN BRIDGE

The pride of Germantown, Ohio, is its old covered bridge, which is the only remaining example of a pure iron inverted bowstring truss covered bridge in the world. The trusses can be viewed from inside or outside the bridge due to the fact that there is no siding. Built in 1865, it crosses the Little Twin Creek with a single span of 100 feet and is no longer open to automobile traffic. It is located in Germantown on East Center Street.

Johnson Mill/Salt Creek Bridge

1876, W.G. No. 35-60-31
Muskingum County, Ohio
Photo by Brian J. McKee

The Johnson Mill/Salt Creek Bridge is the only remaining example of a pure Warren truss covered bridge in the world today. There are other Warren truss covered bridges, but they have been modified in some way. This one has been well maintained by its owner, the Ohio Historic Bridge Association, which bought it in 1960. The bridge was built in 1876 over the Salt Creek with a single span and measures 87 feet in length. It is presently bypassed and closed to traffic. The location is east of Zanesville on Arch Hill Road, about 2 miles north of US40.

WARREN TRUSS

ROBERTS BRIDGE

1829, W.G. No. 35-68-05
PREBLE COUNTY, OHIO
PHOTO BY BRIAN J. McKEE

The Roberts Covered Bridge is the only remaining double-barreled covered bridge in Ohio and one of six in the entire U.S. Roberts Bridge is also Ohio's oldest remaining covered bridge. Its construction along the Camden-Eaton Turnpike was begun by Orlistus Roberts and then finished by James Campbell after Roberts died. It was nearly lost forever when, on August 5, 1986, someone set it on fire and burned all but the heavy Burr trusses. After much debate and fund-raising within the local community, it was decided to move the remains to a spot in Eaton and rebuild it for historical purposes. It was completely restored in accordance with its original design and dedicated with a formal ceremony in September 1991. The event was attended by hundreds of covered bridge enthusiasts and historians from all over the country, demonstrating the widespread appreciation for this rare 80 foot long bridge. It still crosses the same Seven Mile Creek that it did before being moved; however, it has not been reopened to automobile traffic.

BURR TRUSS

The Manchester Bridge is a simple multiple king-post structure built in 1915, which makes it one of the youngest surviving covered bridges in the state. It is one of four remaining covered spans in Noble County, which once had at least 110 of them, and is the only one now open to traffic. The bridge is in surprisingly good condition considering its remote location, and is obviously well maintained. It sits on cut stone abutments and has a length of 49 feet. Fairly difficult to locate, it crosses the Olive Green Creek in Sharon Township on TR3, a gravel road 2.5 miles south of Olive Green.

MANCHESTER BRIDGE

1915, W.G. No. 35-61-33
NOBLE COUNTY, OHIO
PHOTO BY BRIAN J. McKEE

≥ MULTIPLE KING ≤

POST TRUSS

The Otway Bridge is unusual in a couple of respects. First of all, it has been bypassed with a modern concrete span, but remains open to traffic. Secondly, it has an 80 foot long steel bridge on one end, which spanned a mill race in earlier years. It was built by the Smith Bridge Company of Toledo, Ohio, using their Smith Trusses, and a wooden arch was added to it in 1896. The covered bridge measures 127 feet long and crosses the Brush Creek on the west edge of the town of Otway. A festival is held here every year and the bridge is well maintained by the local citizens, who are very proud of it.

OTWAY BRIDGE

1874, W.G. No. 35-73-15
SCIOTO COUNTY, OHIO
PHOTO BY BRIAN J. MCKEE

SMITH

TRUSS

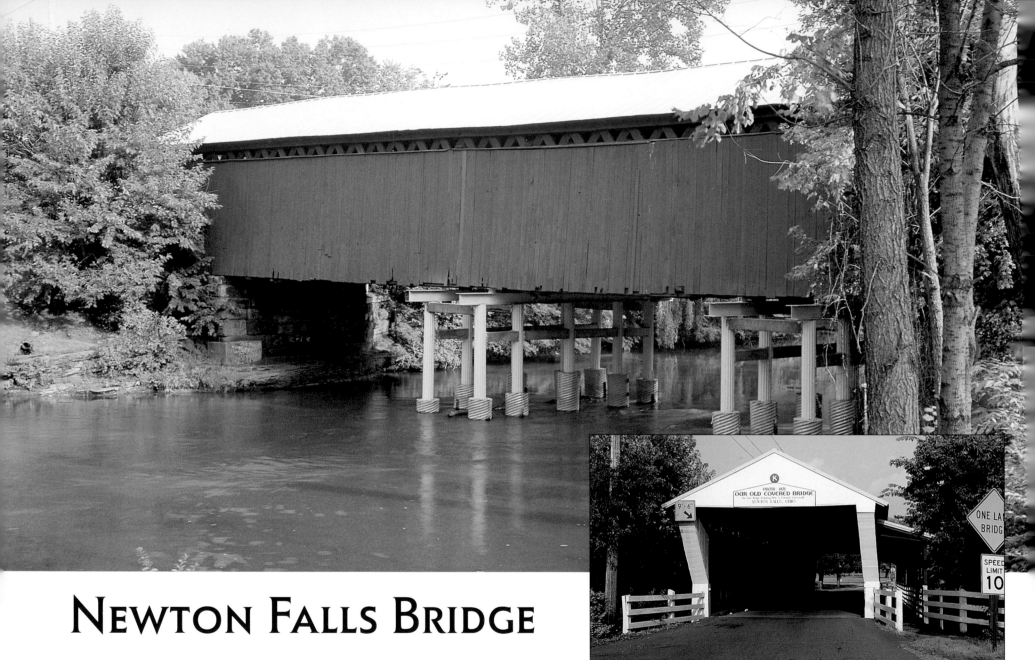

Newton Falls Bridge

The Newton Falls Bridge once had the distinction of being the only covered bridge in Ohio with an external sidewalk, but now there are two in the state, the other being Harpersfield Bridge in Ashtabula County. It is Ohio's second-oldest covered bridge and the oldest still in use by the public. It crosses the east branch of the Mahoning River with a length of 117 feet, and was originally a single-span Town truss bridge, but now is supported with several steel and concrete pylons. The bridge is the pride of the community of Newton Falls, the only town in the U.S. to have a monodigit zip code, 44444.

1831, W.G. No. 35-78-01
TRUMBULL COUNTY, OHIO
PHOTO BY BRIAN J. MCKEE

TOWN
TRUSS

POTTERSBURG BRIDGE

1868, W.G. No. 35-80-01
UNION COUNTY, OHIO
PHOTO BY BRIAN J. McKEE

PARTRIDGE TRUSS

The Pottersburg Bridge is sometimes called the Upper Darby Bridge for the name of the waterway that it crosses: the Big Darby Creek. It is one of only five remaining Partridge truss bridges and is the only one that is unmodified and still open to traffic. Built by Rubin Partridge, the inventor of the truss, it uses one span with a length of 94 feet. Long shaded windows adorn both sides to allow air and light to enter, but restrict the rain and snow to protect the expensive wooden trusses. In 1992, it received a new tin roof, and appears to be kept in excellent condition by the Union County engineer, Steve Stolte. It is located northeast of North Lewisburg on CR164. Union County has four other Partridge truss covered bridges within its boundaries, all of which are open to automobile traffic.

Humpback/Geer's Mill Bridge

MULTIPLE KING

POST TRUSS

1874, W.G. No. 35-82-06
VINTON COUNTY, OHIO
PHOTO BY BRIAN J. MCKEE

The Humpback or Geer's Mill Bridge is sometimes called the Ponn's Bridge and sits in a quiet, scenic valley in southern Vinton County. It replaced an earlier span called Barnes Mill Bridge after it was burned by an arsonist in 1874. The contract for the new bridge was given to Martin McGrath and Lyman Wells of McArthur, Ohio, for $1898. Upon observation of the Humpback Bridge, visitors will realize where it gets this name—it has an unusual amount of positive camber. It crosses the Raccoon Creek with three spans supported by cut stone abutments and two stone piers. Built with the multiple king-post truss system and an additional arch in the center span, it measures 165 feet in length. It is fairly difficult to find in this remote area of southern Ohio, but it is well worth the effort. From Wilkesville, go west on CR8, then right on TR7, then left (south) on TR4 to the bridge.

Shinn Bridge

The Shinn Bridge spans the west branch of the Wolf Creek in Palmer township. It was originally built in 1886 with the multiple king-post truss system and has an arch for additional support. The structure has one span and measures 98 feet in length. Due to damage to its lower chords by an overweight truck, it is presently closed to traffic; however, repairs are being considered. It is located southwest of Wolf Creek on TR447.

MULTIPLE KING
POST TRUSS

1886, W.G. No. 35-84-03
WASHINGTON COUNTY, OHIO
PHOTO BY BRIAN J. McKEE

PARKER BRIDGE

In May of 1991, the Parker Bridge had a near encounter with extinction when it was purposely set on fire by vandals. The southern half burned and fell into the Sandusky River, where it laid for a few days, until James Morris, the Wyandot County engineer, had his crew raise the remaining northern half out of the river and support it with steel piers. The community formed the "Cross Over the Bridge, Again" committee and raised funds to rebuild their old historic landmark. It was completed by the William Morton Construction Co. of Bucyrus, Ohio, and formally dedicated on October 25, 1992. Originally built in 1876 by Weymouth and Bope at a cost of $16.37 per linear foot, it uses a single-span Howe truss system. Measuring 172 feet, it is Ohio's second longest single-span covered bridge, and is open to automobile traffic. The bridge can be located in a scenic valley on Crane TR40, about 3 miles north of Upper Sandusky, and 1 mile west of OH67.

1876, W.G. No. 35-88-03
WYANDOT COUNTY, OHIO
PHOTO BY BRIAN J. McKEE

HOWE
TRUSS

Once... The Most!

Ohio once had more of these than any other state... Covered Bridges! A conservative guess is that we once had over 2000. The national leader today is Pennsylvania, but our remaining covered bridges are treasured artifacts from the past that grace some of our roads. Four covered bridges can be seen while driving along this scenic byway (SR 26). If you have the time, stop at each bridge to learn more about this unique part of Ohio's cultural heritage.

The Hills Covered Bridge

The Hills Covered Bridge was built in 1878 by the Hocking Valley Bridge Works and features a **Howe truss**.

What is a Truss?

A truss is an arrangement of members (posts, rods, timbers, etc.) in a rigid form so united that they support each other plus whatever weight is put upon the whole. Covered bridge trusses employ a triangle or a series of combined triangles. Different bridge designers used different truss designs. Here are some of the truss designs you can see used on the covered bridges found along SR 26.

Covered Bridge Scenic Byway

WAYNE National Forest

HILL'S BRIDGE

The Hill's Bridge, or Hildreth Bridge, as it is sometimes known, is one of several covered bridges that sit near scenic Ohio SR26, north of the historic river town of Marietta. It was built in 1878 using a single-span Howe truss system and measures 122 feet in length. Until recently, it was open to automobile traffic and carried travelers along CR333 over the Little Muskingum River. Today, it is bypassed with a modern bridge and is closed, but is well maintained. A historical marker was placed next to it by the U.S. Forestry Service in 1994.

1878, W.G. No. 35-84-24
WASHINGTON COUNTY, OHIO
PHOTO BY BRIAN J. McKEE

HOWE TRUSS

CAVITT CREEK BRIDGE

HOWE TRUSS

1943, W.G. No. 37-10-06
DOUGLAS COUNTY, OREGON
PHOTO BY SHIMA YOSHIO

The Cavitt Creek Bridge was built in 1943 by Floyd C. Frear, making it a relatively new covered bridge; however, it still utilizes the same wooden Howe trusses of its older counterparts. It gets its name from Robert Cavitt, an early settler along the Little River. The boxed-in windows give the side walls a look of great thickness and strength, which it needs to carry heavy logging trucks. Steel approach ramps connect each end of the bridge to the roadway and the structure itself sits on steel and concrete piers. It stretches across the sparkling Little River with a length of 70 feet on Cavitt Creek Road (CR82A), southeast of Glide.

GOODPASTURE BRIDGE

The brightly painted white Goodpasture Bridge stands out against the dark green background of the Oregon landscape, with its vented windows giving it a distinctive feeling of quality. It was constructed in 1938 using the Howe truss design and spans the McKenzie River with a length of 165 feet. Rebuilt completely in 1987, the Goodpasture Bridge still carries traffic on Goodpasture Road on the west edge of Vida.

1938, W.G. No. 37-20-10
LANE COUNTY, OREGON
PHOTO BY SHIMA YOSHIO

Pengra Bridge

The Howe trusses of the Pengra Bridge use very long one-piece upper and lower chords that had to be shaped with hand tools before they could be finish cut because they were too large for a mill to handle. The lower chord measures 16 inches by 18 inches by 126 feet and the upper chord is 14 inches by 18 inches by 98 feet. The bridge takes its name from the pioneer and surveyor B.J. Pengra, who settled in Oregon in the middle of the nineteenth century. Built in 1938 to replace a previous bridge located just upstream, it crosses the Fall Creek with its 120 foot Howe truss structure. It is closed today, but one can still see it along Place Road, a few miles southeast of Jasper.

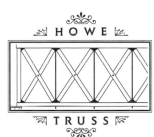

HOWE

TRUSS

1938, W.G. No. 37-20-15
LANE COUNTY, OREGON
PHOTO BY SHIMA YOSHIO

CHITWOOD BRIDGE

The Chitwood Bridge is located in what once was a community bustling with activity, but today, the town of Chitwood consists only of the remains of old boarded-up stores. The bridge, which was built in 1930, still carries traffic across the Yaquina River. It uses a Howe truss system measuring 96 feet long, and has a 33 foot approach on each side. In 1983, it was extensively renovated by John Gilliland. Chitwood is located 11 miles east of Toledo on US20, then right at Chitwood Road.

HOWE

TRUSS

1930, W.G. No. 37-21-03
LINCOLN COUNTY, OREGON
PHOTO BY SHIMA YOSHIO

GILKEY BRIDGE

The Gilkey Bridge was built in 1939 utilizing the single-span Howe truss design, and has a length of 120 feet. One of many covered bridges to cross the Thomas Creek, it was named after the small town of Gilkey Station, which is all but a memory today. The Gilkey Bridge shows more of its truss work than usual, but the bottom portions are boxed in to protect them from the elements. It is located on CR629 southwest of Scio.

H O W E

T R U S S

1939, W.G. No. 37-22-04
LINN COUNTY, OREGON
PHOTO BY SHIMA YOSHIO

Gallon House Bridge

The Gallon House Bridge takes its name from a former liquor house that was located nearby in the pre-prohibition era. It was constructed for $1310 in 1916 using the Howe truss design, and was restored completely in 1990. It crosses the Abiqua River with a single span measuring 84 feet in length. Gallon House Bridge has the distinction of being the oldest Oregon covered bridge still in use. Visitors can find it located northwest of Silverton on Gallon House Road (CR647).

HOWE
TRUSS

1916, W.G. No. 37-24-01
MARION COUNTY, OREGON
PHOTO BY SHIMA YOSHIO

T O W N TRUSS

1854, W.G. No. 38-01-01
ADAMS COUNTY, PENNSYLVANIA
PHOTO BY JEFFREY REICHARD

SAUCK'S BRIDGE

The Sauck's Bridge is a good example of a Town lattice truss system. It was used by the Union troops on their way to Gettysburg before the famous Civil War battle, and was also utilized by the Confederate troops on their retreat from the deadly battlegrounds. Since many wooden covered bridges were burned during the war, it is astonishing that this one survived, given the intensity of the fighting in the area. Built in 1854, Sauck's bridge spans the Marsh Creek and measures 91 feet long. It is not being used at this time, but it is scheduled to be repaired soon. Sauck's Bridge is located by going 1 mile southwest of the historic town of Gettysburg on business route 15 to Pumping Station Road, then making a right turn and going 1.8 miles to Waterworks Road (TR26). Make a left turn and the bridge is a quarter mile ahead.

Author's note: This bridge was washed away by a storm on June 19, 1996. It is uncertain whether it will be rebuilt.

Diehl's/Turner's Bridge

The Diehl's or Turner's Bridge is one of 14 covered bridges remaining in historic Bedford County. Its vertical siding only covers the lower portion of the Burr arch trusses, leaving a large open area for light and ventilation. All exposed wood is painted white for protection against the elements, and the bridge, which is 87 feet long, is very well maintained. It still carries automobile traffic across the Raystown Branch of the Juniata River, as it has for the past 104 years. It can be found west of Mann's Choice on TR418, and also can be seen on the south side of the Pennsylvania Turnpike at milepost 136.

BURR TRUSS

1892, W.G. No. 38-05-19
BEDFORD COUNTY, PENNSYLVANIA
PHOTO BY THOMAS E. WALCZAK

The Jackson Mill Bridge was named after the old grist mill that sits next to it. These mill and bridge combinations were a common scene in the nineteenth century, but very few remain today. Originally built in 1889 with the Burr truss, it has a single span and measures 96 feet in length. Because it was moved to a wider crossing along the river several years ago, a two-span open king-post truss approach bridge was added to one end. In 1993, the bridge was disassembled and completely restored. It crosses the Brush Creek in East Providence Township, on TR412, which is southwest of Breezewood.

JACKSON MILL BRIDGE

1889, W.G. No. 38-05-25
BEDFORD COUNTY, PENNSYLVANIA
PHOTO BY BRIAN J. McKEE

BURR

TRUSS

WERTZ/RED BRIDGE

The Wertz or Red Bridge crosses the Tulpehocken Creek with a 218 foot long single-span Burr truss system. It is the longest surviving single-span covered bridge in the state and ranks third in the U.S. Built in 1869 for a cost of $7650, it is covered with horizontal siding with a full-length vent just under the roof line. It sits on stone and mortar abutments. The stone wingwalls and parapets are typical of many of the covered bridges in the northeastern U.S.; however, its "stepped" or "store front" portal design is unique to just a few remaining Pennsylvania covered bridges. In 1979, it was listed on the National Register of Historic Places. No longer open to automobile traffic, the Wertz Bridge is located west of Reading on TR291 in the Tulpehocken Creek Valley Park.

1869, W.G. No. 38-06-06
BERKS COUNTY, PENNSYLVANIA
PHOTO BY RODNEY AND CONNIE NOLDER

BURR

TRUSS

1869, W.G. No. 38-06-07
BERKS COUNTY, PENNSYLVANIA
PHOTO BY BRIAN J. McKEE

DREIBELBIS STATION BRIDGE

The Dreibelbis Station Bridge is one of very few covered bridges remaining with a "stepped" or "store front" portal design. It ranks as the longest single-span covered bridge in the state still open to traffic (Wertz/Red Bridge is longer, but is closed to traffic) and crosses the Maiden Creek by using a 190 foot Burr truss system. Full-length windows run down both sides of the bridge to allow for additional light and ventilation. Massive stone wing walls and parapets lead travelers into the bridge in a style typical of many Pennsylvania covered bridges. It is located south of Lenhartsville, just off the east side of PA143 on TR745.

BURR TRUSS

1987, W.G. No. 38-15-13

CHESTER COUNTY, PENNSYLVANIA

PHOTO BY BRIAN J. MCKEE

KENNEDY BRIDGE

The Kennedy Bridge is unique in the fact that it was built with a special type of extremely hard wood called Bongossi wood from Africa. This type of wood was used for its fire- and insect-resistant properties as well as its strength. Originally constructed with the Burr truss system in 1856, it was burned and destroyed in 1987. This new exact replica was built in its place and even retains the rare stepped portal design. The bridge spans the French Creek and measures 120 feet in length. It is one of 15 covered bridges located in Chester County, and can be found north of Kimberton on TR522.

McGee's Mill Bridge

The last remaining covered bridge in Clearfield County, McGee's Mills Bridge was nearly lost during the winter of 1994 when heavy snows proved too much of a load, collapsing the roof and damaging the Burr trusses. It was rebuilt about a year later and is now open to automobile traffic. The wide portal edges are unusual and also hide the laminated wooden beams inside, which were added to give the bridge more load capacity. Originally built in 1873, it is unique in the fact that it is the last covered bridge to cross any part of the Susquehanna River. This one crosses the west branch with a 116 foot single span and is located at McGee's Mills on TR322.

BURR

TRUSS

1873, W.G. No. 38-17-01
CLEARFIELD COUNTY, PENNSYLVANIA
PHOTO BY THOMAS E. WALCZAK

LOGAN MILLS BRIDGE

The Logan Mills Bridge was built in 1874 to give farmers access to the Logan Mill on the north side of the Big Fishing Creek. Using a low queen-post truss system to span the creek, it measures 63 feet in length and still carries automobile traffic as well as a large number of Amish horse-drawn vehicles. The old mill is still here, too, and the scene of the two together takes the visitor back into the nineteenth century. They are located 5 miles west of Loganton on PA800, and then a half mile south on SR2007.

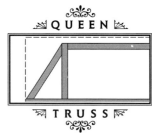

QUEEN
TRUSS

1874, W.G. No. 38-18-01
CLINTON COUNTY, PENNSYLVANIA
PHOTO BY THOMAS E. WALCZAK

One of 24 covered bridges in Columbia County, the Wanich Bridge is a fine example of a Burr truss system. It is also one of 10 such Burr structures located in the county; the rest being queen-post trusses. Built by George Russell, Jr. in 1884, it spans the Little Fishing Creek and measures 108 feet in length. It sits on stone and mortar abutments that have been reinforced with concrete. An unusual feature of the Wanich Bridge is that its siding runs vertically on one side and horizontally on the other. It is located on the Hemlock/Mt. Pleasant Township line about 2 miles northwest of Bloomsburg on PA42, then east a quarter mile on TR493.

WANICH BRIDGE

1884, W.G. No. 38-19-18
COLUMBIA COUNTY, PENNSYLVANIA
PHOTO BY BRIAN J. McKEE

BURR
TRUSS

Martin's Mill Bridge is sometimes called the Shindle Bridge and has the distinction of being the longest remaining covered bridge in the state built with the Town truss system, and the second longest overall. Originally built by Jacob Shirk, a local contractor, it measures 225 feet as it crosses the Conococheague Creek with two spans. It is supported by two stone abutments and a stone center pier, and has stone wing walls and parapets. The roof is covered with over 15,000 cedar shingles and there are four windows on each side. In 1972, the bridge was nearly lost when it was swept off its abutments by flood waters from Hurricane Agnes. Beginning in 1993, it was completely restored by the Martin's Mill Covered Bridge Association. It was opened to traffic for a dedication ceremony in August 1995, then closed again. A striking feature of this bridge is the "store front" or "stepped" portal design, which adds to its majestic appearance. It is located southwest of Greencastle on TR341 (Weaver Road).

MARTIN'S MILL BRIDGE

1849 W.G. No. 38-28-01
FRANKLIN COUNTY, PENNSYLVANIA
PHOTO BY BRIAN J. McKEE

TOWN

TRUSS

The St. Mary's Bridge, or Shade Gap Bridge, as it is sometimes called, is the last remaining covered bridge in Huntingdon County. The St. Mary's Church sits across the highway from the bridge and the two together make a picturesque rural scene. The bridge is in excellent condition and has been reinforced with steel to allow for heavier loads. Built with the Howe truss system, it has red siding covering only the lower portion of the white trusses, in a similar style to the covered bridges in Bedford County. It crosses the Shade Creek with a length of 65 feet and sits on two concrete abutments. One can find this bridge easily by taking US522 about 3 miles northwest of Shade Gap, then making a right turn on TR358.

St. Mary's Bridge

1889, W.G. No. 38-31-01
Huntingdon County, Pennsylvania
Photo by Brian J. McKee

HOWE

TRUSS

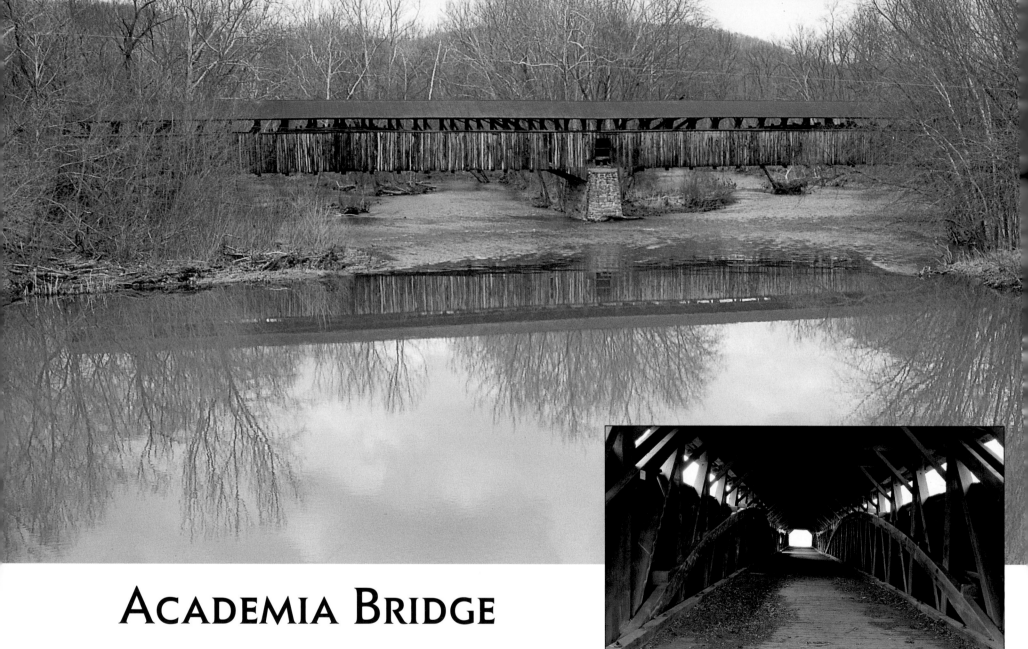

ACADEMIA BRIDGE

The Academia Bridge is also known as the Pomeroy Bridge, and is Pennsylvania's longest surviving covered bridge, at a length of 278 feet. It was built by James Groninger using the Burr truss system and sits on stone abutments and a stone center pier. It also has stone wing walls and parapets, which is a typical building feature of many of the covered bridges in Pennsylvania. Closed and bypassed, it seems to be abandoned as it crosses the Tuscarora Creek with two spans. The bridge is under ownership of the Juniata County Historical Society. It is located on the Beale and Spruce Hill Township line, on the southeast edge of Academia on SR3013.

1901, W.G. No. 38-34-01
JUNIATA COUNTY, PENNSYLVANIA
PHOTO BY BRIAN J. McKEE

BURR
TRUSS

Rose Hill/Wenger's Bridge

BURR TRUSS

1849, W.G. No. 38-36-14
LANCASTER COUNTY, PENNSYLVANIA
PHOTO BY BRIAN J. MCKEE

The Rose Hill or Wenger's Bridge is sometimes referred to as the Zook's Mill Bridge. It is tied for the third oldest covered bridge in Lancaster County, an area well known for its outstanding inventory of 28 authentic wooden truss covered bridges. Using the Burr truss system, Henry Zook built this single-span bridge across the Cocalico Creek on the Ephrata/Warwick Township line. It measures 89 feet in length and is 15 feet wide. Massive stone abutments support the ends while stone wing walls and parapets contain the earth along the riverbank. Rose Hill Bridge is still open to traffic and is located west of Brownstown. To find it, take PA272 1 mile south of Brownstown, then turn right on Rose Hill Road. Go a half mile, then turn left on TR797.

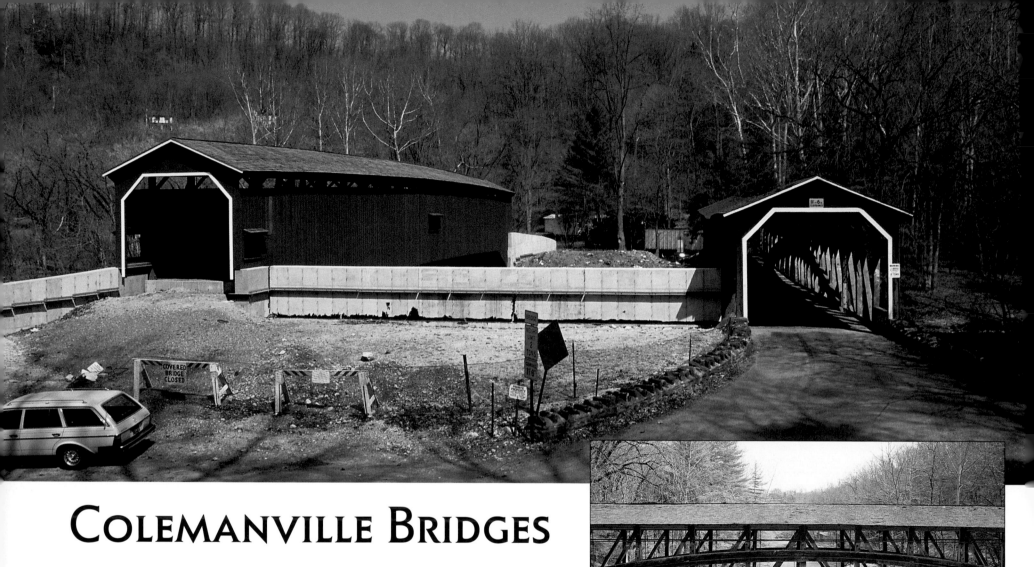

Colemanville Bridges

The first Colemanville Bridge was built in 1856 by James C. Carpenter using the Burr truss system. It lived a somewhat rough life as it was swept off its abutments on at least two occasions by flood waters and then reinstalled after both events. In 1990, after it was determined that the old bridge was rotted beyond repair, a new covered bridge was constructed just 75 feet downstream from the original one. The new bridge was built with all new wood and sits on concrete abutments. It is also 5 feet higher that the original bridge to avoid the flood problems of the past. Bridge buffs rarely have the opportunity to see two covered bridges so close together, and they are usually in an end-to-end arrangement. The two Colemanville Bridges, being side by side, represented a once-in-a-lifetime scene that may never be duplicated. The old bridge was removed in 1994. The new bridge measures 167 feet and is located over Penguin Creek west of Martic Forge on PA324, then left on Fox Hollow Road (TR428).

1856 & 1990,
W.G. No. 38-36-26 and 38-36-57
Lancaster County, Pennsylvania
Photo by Brian J. McKee

BURR
TRUSS

A subject of one of the most beautiful scenes in the state of Pennsylvania, the McConnell's Mill Bridge sits next to the old McConnell's Grist Mill and Dam, which are operated by the state. The bridge was built in 1874, and is one of only four in the state of Pennsylvania to use the Howe truss system. It is still used extensively by automobile traffic as it crosses the Slippery Rock Creek with a single span of 101 feet. Both the bridge and mill are well maintained and can be easily found in the McConnell's Mill State Park, an area that has been designated a National Natural Landmark. The park is located about 7 miles east of New Castle on the south side of US422.

McConnell's Mill Bridge

1874, W.G. No. 38-37-01
Lawrence County, Pennsylvania
Photo by Thomas E. Walczak

HOWE

TRUSS

Sam Wagner/Gottlieb Brown Bridge

The Sam Wagner or Gottlieb Brown Bridge spans the Chillisquaque Creek about 1 mile northeast of the rural community of Pottsgrove. This 86 foot Burr arch truss bridge joins together two counties in this quiet farming area and is a pleasant diversion from the hectic traffic on I-80 just a half mile to the north. It was reportedly built for $939 by George W. Keefer.

1881, W.G. No. 38-47-01/49-11
MONTOUR-NORTHUMBERLAND
COUNTIES, PENNSYLVANIA
PHOTO BY THOMAS E. WALCZAK

BURR
TRUSS

The Longdon L. Miller Bridge is typical of the style of covered bridge built in Washington County in the late 1800s and early 1900s. There are 24 existing covered bridges in this county and all are similar in appearance, with red vertical siding and metal roofs. The Miller Bridge uses a queen-post truss to support it across the Templeton Fork of the Wheeling Creek in West Finley Township. It measures 77 feet long and almost 12 feet wide, making it the longest covered bridge in the county. Like many of the Washington County covered bridges, it has several additional supports under it in the creek bed. To find the bridge, take SR3037 south from West Finley to SR4016/3026, then turn left and go to TR414. Turn left and go forward to the bridge.

LONGDON L. MILLER BRIDGE

DATE UNKNOWN, W.G. NO. 38-63-22
WASHINGTON COUNTY, PENNSYLVANIA
PHOTO BY BRIAN J. MCKEE

QUEEN

TRUSS

Photo sign reads: BELLS 1850 MILLS / DANIEL McCAIN / ARCHITECT & CONTRACTOR

BELL'S MILL BRIDGE

Bell's Mill Bridge was built in 1850 by Daniel McCain, making it one of Pennsylvania's oldest surviving covered bridges. It uses a single-span Burr truss to cross the Sewickley Creek and measures 107 feet in length. In 1988 it was extensively restored and remains open to automobile traffic today. The Greek Revival design of the portals is a unique feature of this bridge, which is located on SR3061, about 3 miles northeast of West Newton.

1850, W.G. No. 38-65-01
WESTMORELAND COUNTY, PENNSYLVANIA
PHOTO BY THOMAS E. WALCZAK

BURR TRUSS

CAMPBELL BRIDGE

1909, W.G. No. 40-23-02
GREENVILLE COUNTY, SOUTH CAROLINA
PHOTO BY SHIMA YOSHIO

The Campbell Bridge is South Carolina's only remaining wooden covered bridge. It was built in 1909 using the Howe truss system and crosses the Beaver Dam with a length of 41 feet. Visitors can locate it southwest of Gowensville on Pleasant Hill Road.

ELIZABETHTON BRIDGE

The Elizabethton Bridge's unusual hip roof design sets it apart from most other covered bridges. It was constructed in 1882 with the Howe truss system. Still open to light traffic, it crosses the Doe River with a single span measuring 134 feet in length. Elizabethton is the Carter County seat, and you can find this bridge on Third Street between Main Street and Riverside Drive.

1882, W.G. NO. 42-10-01
CARTER COUNTY, TENNESSEE
PHOTO BY THOMAS E. WALCZAK

HOWE
TRUSS

PULP MILL BRIDGE

BURR TRUSS

CI820, W. G. NO. 45-01-04
ADDISON COUNTY, VERMONT
PHOTO BY BRIAN J. MCKEE

The Pulp Mill Bridge is one of the nation's oldest surviving bridges, and amazingly is still used daily for public automobile transportation. It is also one of only six remaining double-barrel covered bridges in the country, with its third Burr truss running down the center and dividing the two lanes of traffic. Originally, a single-span bridge, it now crosses the Otter Creek with two additional center piers for added strength. It measures 199 feet in length and connects the towns of Middlebury and Weybridge on Pulp Mill Bridge Road.

The Rutland Railroad Bridge, also known as the East Shoreham Bridge, has spanned the Lemon Fair River at the Richville Pond for the past 99 years and still appears to be in excellent condition. The 108 foot long structure uses the strong Howe truss system, common in many railroad bridges, for its main support. The old railroad line has been abandoned since 1951, and now the bridge serves only pedestrian traffic. It is located southeast of Shoreham Center off of East Shoreham Road at a parking area on the west side. A large historical marker has been placed here for the benefit of bridge visitors, who must make a pleasant hike about a quarter mile down the old railroad grade to actually see the structure itself.

RUTLAND RAILROAD BRIDGE

1897, W.G. No. 45-01-05
ADDISON COUNTY, VERMONT
PHOTO BY BRIAN J. MCKEE

HOWE TRUSS

PAPER MILL BRIDGE

TOWN TRUSS

1889, W.G. No. 45-02-03
BENNINGTON COUNTY, VERMONT
PHOTO BY TOM HILDRETH

The Paper Mill Bridge is the longest remaining covered bridge in Bennington County at 125.5 feet. It uses the Town lattice truss system to cross the Walloomsac River with a single span. Recently, it was bypassed with a temporary steel bridge since it was determined that it was no longer safe for vehicular traffic. It is also interesting to note that this is one of very few covered bridges in the state of Vermont to have painted siding. A waterfall under it makes a beautiful scene for artists and photographers. It is located just off VT67A on Murphy Road.

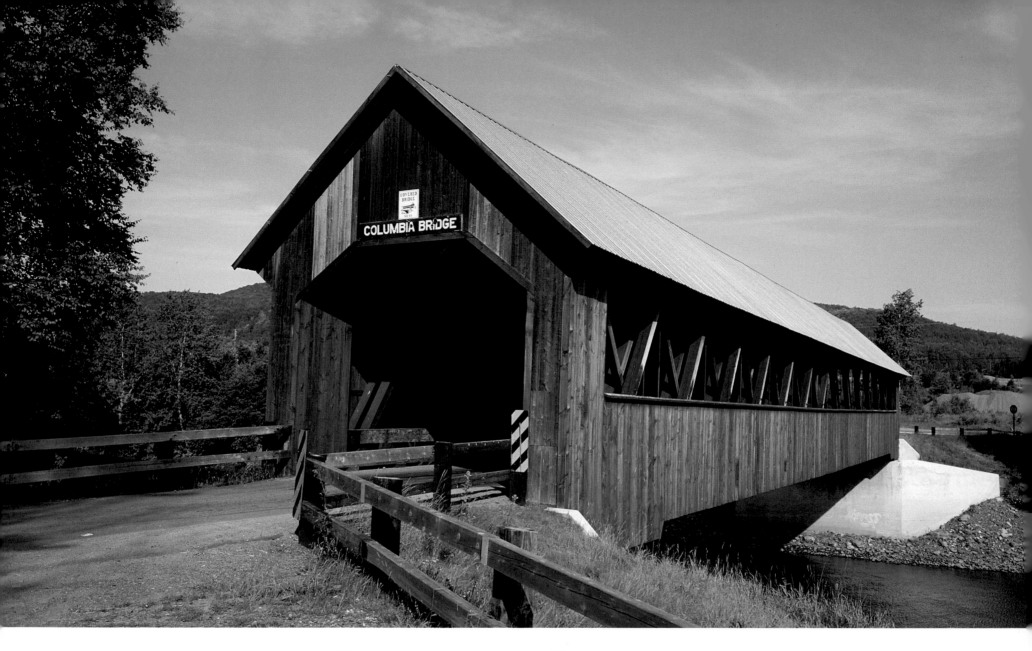

COLUMBIA BRIDGE

1912, W.G. No. 29-04-07 or 45-05-02

COOS COUNTY, NEW HAMPSHIRE AND
ESSEX COUNTY, VERMONT

PHOTO BY THOMAS E. WALCZAK

The Columbia Bridge is one of only three covered bridges remaining that join two states together. Originally built in 1912, it crosses the Connecticut River with a 146 foot long Howe truss. The south side of the bridge is completely sided, while the other is only sided halfway up. It is open to automobile traffic and is well kept. Columbia Bridge is located just west of US3, about 4 miles southwest of Colebrook, New Hampshire.

HOWE TRUSS

WEST DUMMERSTON BRIDGE

TOWN

TRUSS

The West Dummerston Bridge was built by Caleb B. Lamson using a two-span Town lattice truss system. At 265 feet long, it is Vermont's second-longest covered bridge, with Scott's Bridge being the longest. It crosses the West River in the town of Dummerston just east of VT30 on East West Road. The bridge is currently closed for repairs and a temporary bridge has been installed to handle local traffic.

1872, W.G. No. 45-13-02
WINDHAM COUNTY, VERMONT
PHOTO BY BRIAN J. MCKEE

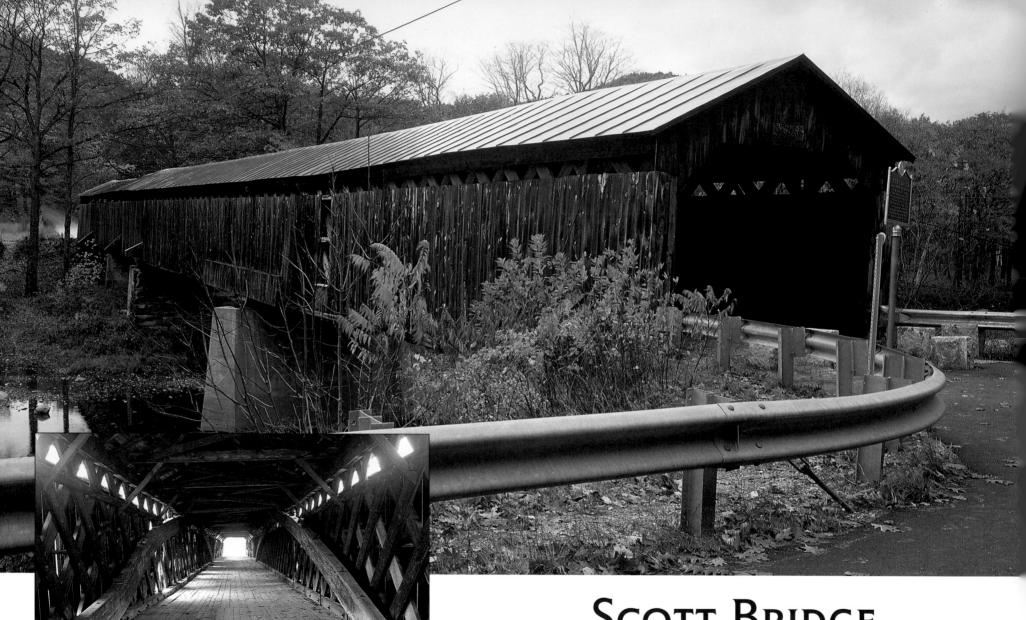

SCOTT BRIDGE

1870, W.G. No. 45-13-13
WINDHAM COUNTY, VERMONT
PHOTO BY BRIAN J. McKEE

TOWN TRUSS

The Scott Bridge was originally built by Harrison Chamberlain using the Town lattice truss system. At that time, it measured 166 feet long and was the longest single-span covered bridge in Vermont. Two king-post truss sections were added to the structure at later dates as the river bank eroded due to flooding. Now, it measures 277 feet and has the distinction of being the longest surviving covered bridge in the state. No longer open to traffic, it crosses the West River with three spans on the west side of VT30, just below the Townshend Reservoir and Dam.

DOWNERS/UPPER FALLS BRIDGE

The Downers or Upper Falls Bridge was built in 1851 using the Town lattice truss system. It crosses the Black River with a single span and measures 121 feet in length. One of the abutments is concrete and the other is natural stone. The naturally weathered vertical wood siding has turned into an array of colors over the years, giving the bridge a artistic appearance. It was restored in 1976 by the famed covered bridge builders Milton Graton & Sons. Downers Bridge is located in the town of Weathersfield, just south of VT131 on Upper Falls Road.

TOWN TRUSS

1840, W.G. No. 45-14-08
WINDSOR COUNTY, VERMONT
PHOTO BY BRIAN J. McKEE

MULTIPLE KING

POST TRUSS

1836, W.G. No. 45-14-12
WINDSOR COUNTY, VERMONT
PHOTO BY BRIAN J. McKEE

TAFTSVILLE BRIDGE

The Taftsville Bridge is Vermont's fourth-longest covered bridge, measuring 190 feet as it crosses the Ottauquechee River at Taftsville. It was built by Solomon Emmons with a two-span multiple king-post/queen-post truss with an arch, reinforced with iron rods, and is still open to automobile traffic. According to the latest records, it is tied for the second-oldest covered bridge in Vermont; the Pulp Mill Bridge is the oldest. From the riverbed, the bridge and roaring dam behind it make a beautiful scene, which attracts artists and photographers from around the world. It is located just off US4 on River Road.

Cornish/Windsor Bridge

At 450 feet in length, the magnificent Cornish/Windsor Bridge is the longest remaining wooden covered bridge in use in the United States, today. It is a site to behold as it stretches across the Connecticut River, joining the states of New Hampshire and Vermont. Using the Town lattice truss system, it takes only two spans supported by a single center pier to cross the river. It was built in 1866, in an era when there were several covered bridges over the Connecticut River. Today, only three such spans survive. In 1989, it was extensively restored and reopened to automobile traffic. Since the restoration, it is capable of carrying two lanes of traffic and heavy vehicles such as school buses and fire trucks, and also has night lighting inside. In 1970, it was named a National Historic Civil Engineering Landmark. Visitors will find it easy to locate on the east edge of Windsor, Vermont.

TOWN TRUSS

1866, W.G. No. 29-10-09/45-14-14
SULLIVAN COUNTY, NH &
WINDSOR COUNTY, VT
PHOTO BY BRIAN J. MCKEE

The Humpback Bridge of Virginia is one of the nation's most unique bridges in the fact that it has such a large amount of positive camber in its trusses, giving the bridge a distinct "humped" appearance. Closed and bypassed since 1929, it is now a historical monument surrounded by a public park. It uses a single-span multiple king-post truss system measuring 100 feet long, and sits on two cut stone abutments over Dunlap Creek in Covington Township. The wooden truss members were hand hewn as one can see from the rough cuts and notches still in them. Originally a part of the James River Kanawha Turnpike in 1835, Humpback Bridge is now designated a Virginia Historic Landmark. It is located west of Covington on US60, then just south on VA600 at the wayside park.

HUMPBACK BRIDGE

1857, W.G. No. 46-03-01
ALLEGHANY COUNTY, VIRGINIA
PHOTO BY BRIAN J. MCKEE

MULTIPLE KING

POST TRUSS

GRAY'S RIVER BRIDGE

HOWE

TRUSS

1905, W.G. No. 47-35-01

WAHKIAKUM COUNTY, WASHINGTON

PHOTO BY SHIMA YOSHIO

The Gray's River Bridge is distinctive because of its unusual portal design. It was originally built in 1905, then so extensively rebuilt in 1989 that the present structure is actually considered a new bridge. Using the two-span Howe truss design, it crosses the Gray's River with a length of 158 feet. It is located south of Grays River on Covered Bridge Road.

Colfax/Road Bridge

The Colfax Bridge started life in 1922 as a railroad bridge, and was later converted to automobile traffic. Today, it is privately owned but still in use. It crosses the Palouse River with a single-span Howe truss system measuring 163 feet in length. It is located by going 4.7 miles northwest of Colfax on Green Hollow Road, then 0.7 miles left on Manning Road, and 0.3 miles left on the old railroad grade at Manning.

1922, W.G. No. 47-38-01
Whitman County, Washington
Photo by Shima Yoshio

HOWE TRUSS

The Fletcher Bridge is one of two remaining covered bridges in Harrison County, and despite being located on an abandoned road, it is still open and is used sparingly. It is typical of a style of bridge used in West Virginia during the nineteenth century, making use of the multiple king-post truss system. It sits on dry laid cut stone abutments and has a length of 62 feet. The bridge was built for $1372 by William J. Williams and the abutments by L.E. Sturm. Fletcher Bridge is located in Ten Mile Township over the Ten Mile Creek. To find it, take CR5 about 1.5 miles north of US50, then go left on CR5/29.

FLETCHER BRIDGE

1891, W.G. No. 48-17-03
HARRISON COUNTY, WEST VIRGINIA
PHOTO BY BRIAN J. McKEE

MULTIPLE KING

POST TRUSS

PHILIPPI BRIDGE

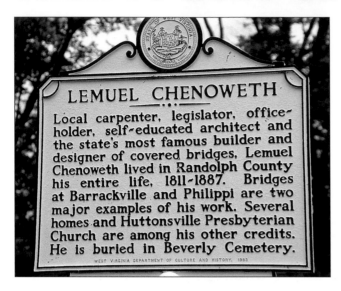

LEMUEL CHENOWETH

Local carpenter, legislator, office-holder, self-educated architect and the state's most famous builder and designer of covered bridges, Lemuel Chenoweth lived in Randolph County his entire life, 1811-1887. Bridges at Barrackville and Philippi are two major examples of his work. Several homes and Huttonsville Presbyterian Church are among his other credits. He is buried in Beverly Cemetery.

WEST VIRGINIA DEPARTMENT OF CULTURE AND HISTORY, 1983

The Philippi Bridge has the distinction of being the longest remaining double-barreled covered bridge in the nation. Measuring 304 feet, it crosses the Tygart Valley River with a two-span Long truss with wooden arches. It was originally built with one cut stone center pier, then two additional concrete piers were added in 1938. A steel and concrete floor were also added in 1938 to provide more capacity for the growing number of heavy vehicles. Today, it is the only covered bridge that carries traffic on a U.S. federal highway. It was built by Lemuel and Eli Chenoweth for $12,181.24, a cost that pales in comparison to the $1.3 million that it took to rebuild it after a disastrous fire in February 1989. Today, it is also one of the few covered bridges that is equipped with a fire alarm and sprinkler system. Over the years, it has undergone several changes in appearance, and during the last rebuild, it was painstakingly restored to its original look of 1852.

1852, W.G. No. 48-01-01
BARBOUR COUNTY, WEST VIRGINIA
PHOTO BY BRIAN J. McKEE

LONG TRUSS

BARRACKVILLE BRIDGE

The Barrackville Bridge is one of the finest examples of nineteenth-century wooden truss bridge construction in the country. Built by famed bridge craftsmen Lemuel and Eli Chenoweth for $12.50 per linear foot, the Barrackville Bridge carried travelers on the Fairmont-Wheeling Turnpike across the Buffalo Creek for more than 134 years. Closed and bypassed in 1987, it is currently undergoing restoration by the state of West Virginia. It uses the Burr truss system and measures 145 feet, 9 inches long, which makes it the longest single-span covered bridge in the state. It is also the second oldest in the state, a rare survivor of the destruction of the Civil War. A sidewalk was added to the bridge in 1934, but was removed during the current project. The bridge sits on dry laid cut stone abutments into which the ends of the Burr arches rest. Barrackville Bridge is easy to find on the north edge of Barrackville on WV250/32.

BURR TRUSS

1853, W.G. No. 48-25-02
MARION COUNTY, WEST VIRGINIA
PHOTO BY BRIAN J. MCKEE

LOCUST CREEK BRIDGE

The Locust Creek Bridge is the only known example of a double intersection Warren truss covered bridge in existence. It was built by R.N. Bruce for $1325 and was open to traffic until 1990, when it was closed and bypassed with a new concrete bridge. Sitting in a quiet, rural valley, it measures 113 feet long and 14 feet wide, and sits on two fascinating dry stone abutments. It has naturally weathered vertical siding and a bright metal roof. The location of this unique bridge is 6 miles south west of Hillsboro on CR31 in Little Levels Township.

1853, W.G. No. 48-25-02
MARION COUNTY, WEST VIRGINIA
PHOTO BY BRIAN J. McKEE

WARREN
TRUSS

HUNDRED/FISH CREEK BRIDGE

Little history has been recorded about this short but very functional bridge located in Church Township in West Virginia's northwest corner. It is still open to traffic, despite having to be repaired quite often due to damage inflicted by oversized trucks. Measuring only 36 feet in length and 13 feet wide, it uses a king-post truss and sits on dry laid cut stone abutments. There is a narrow air vent along the top of its vertical siding and it has a corrugated tin roof. The Hundred or Fish Creek Bridge is located at the south edge of the town of Hundred, just off US250 on CR13.

1881, W.G. No. 48-52-01
WETZEL COUNTY, WEST VIRGINIA
PHOTO BY BRIAN J. MCKEE

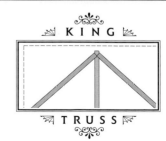

KING
TRUSS

Town Truss

CEDARBURG BRIDGE

1876, W.G. No. 49-46-01

Ozaukee County, Wisconsin

Photo by Shima Yoshio

Built in 1876, the Cedarburg Bridge is the state of Wisconsin's last remaining old covered bridge. The county maintains the structure even though it is no longer used by automobile traffic. It spans the Cedar Creek with a single-span 120 foot Town lattice truss system and has a center pier added for additional load capacity. It is located at the north edge of Cedarburg on Covered Bridge Road.

HARTLAND BRIDGE

HOWE TRUSS

1899, W.G. No. 55-02-07
CARLETON COUNTY, NEW BRUNSWICK
PHOTO AND TEXT BY THOMAS E. WALCZAK

The massive Hartland Bridge holds the distinction of being the world's longest surviving wooden covered bridge. Built in 1899 as an uncovered Howe truss bridge, the engineering masterpiece was sided and roofed amid much controversy in the early 1920s. Now beloved and revered for its uniqueness, it stretches 1282 feet (391 meters) in seven spans across the St. John River at Hartland. This famous tourist attraction has withstood many encounters with fire, floods, high winds, and auto accidents over the years, and still serves public transportation today. It is located at Hartland, just off NB103 on Hartland Bridge Hill Road.

ASHNOLA RIVER ROAD/RED BRIDGE

This unusual and very interesting bridge has its wooden Howe trusses covered but does not have roofing over the floor. The trusses are the most expensive components of a bridge and therefore were given the most protection from the elements of nature. The Ashnola River Road Bridge was constructed in 1923 by a subsidiary of the Great Northern Railway Company of Minnesota to facilitate the gold and coal mining companies, but was later converted to a highway bridge. It uses three separate spans to cross the Similkameen River and measures 400 feet in length. A total of nine of this type of wooden bridge were documented, but only this one survives today. It can be found south of Route 3 and west of Keremeos on Ashnola River Road, a short distance from the Washington State border.

⊷ HOWE ⊶

T R U S S

1923, W.G. No. 52-06-02
SIMILKAMEEN DIVISION,
BRITISH COLUMBIA

PHOTO BY SHIMA YOSHIO

CANADA

All covered bridges were commonly referred to as "kissing bridges" in their heyday since they were a good place to steal a kiss from one's partner as they slowly passed through the long dark tunnel. The name stuck with this outstanding 1881 structure that is located at West Montrose on old route 86. Designed and built by John and Benjamin Bear, it measures 190 feet (58 meters) in length, and uses a two-span queen-post truss to support it across the Grand River. Today, it is the only remaining covered bridge on a public highway in the entire province of Ontario.

KISSING BRIDGE

1881, W.G. No. 59-50-01
WATERLOO COUNTY, ONTARIO
PHOTO BY SHIMA YOSHIO

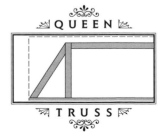

QUEEN

TRUSS

FISHER HILL/McVETTY-McKERRY/GOULD BRIDGE

TOWN TRUSS

1893, W.G. No. 61-18-08
COMPTON COUNTY, QUÉBEC
PHOTO BY GÉRALD ARBOUR

Nineteenth-century bridges were named after the builder, local landowner, river, roadway, or nearby town in most cases, so it is not unusual to see many names attached to one. This outstanding structure crosses the Rivière au Saumon with a two-span Town lattice truss system and is supported with beautiful stone abutments and center pier. At 206 feet (63 meters), it is the longest of the six surviving covered bridges in Compton County. No longer open to automobile traffic, it has been bypassed with a modern bridge. The location is 2.5 miles northwest of Gould along the road to Weedon.

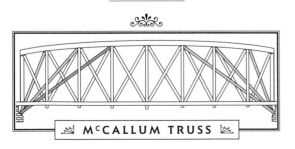

1861, W.G. No. 61-27-01
HUNTINGDON COUNTY, QUÉBEC
PHOTO BY GÉRALD ARBOUR

CANADA

McCALLUM TRUSS

LE PONT COUVERT DE POWERSCOURT

The Powerscourt Covered Bridge (sometimes called the Percy Bridge) has the distinction of being the only remaining example of a McCallum inflexible arched truss in the world, and perhaps the only one ever built on a public roadway. This unique truss was patented by Rochester, New York, native Daniel C. McCallum in 1851 for use on railroad lines. Approximately 150 railroad covered bridges were built in North America using this design. It was difficult to build and required pre-stressing, which caused many bridge builders to choose other, more easily assembled bridge designs, such as the Long and Howe trusses. In 1861, local resident Robert Graham constructed the 180 foot (55 meter) Powerscourt Bridge over the Chateauguay River using two separate McCallum truss spans for a fee of $1675. It originally sat on gravel-filled timber cribs that were later replaced with stone and mortar piers. Today it uses a mixture of stone and concrete piers and abutments, and has approach spans at each end. Observers will immediately notice the curved top chord and roof line of each span, which are unique to this type of truss. The Powerscourt Bridge is the second-oldest surviving covered bridge in Canada, and is located on the west edge of Powerscourt, which is about 1.5 miles north of the U.S. border, and 3 miles west of NY374.

INDEX

DATES LISTED WHEN KNOWN

Contoocook Railroad (1889)	Town	Merrimack	NH-07-07
Rowell's (1853)	Long/arch	Merrimack	NH-07-08
Sulphite Railroad (1896)	Pratt Deck	Merrimack	NH-07-09
New England College (1972)	Town	Merrimack	NH-07-12
Blacksmith Shop (1881)	MKP	Sullivan	NH-10-01
Dingleton (1882)	MKP	Sullivan	NH-10-02
Pier Railroad (1896)	Town	Sullivan	NH-10-03
Wright Railroad (1895)	Town/arch	Sullivan	NH-10-04
Corbin (1994)	Town	Sullivan	NH-10-05 #2
McDermott (1869)	Town/arch	Sullivan	NH-10-06
Drewsville/Prentiss (1869)	Town	Sullivan	NH-10-07
Meriden/Mill (1880)	MKP	Sullivan	NH-10-08
Cornish/Windsor (1866)	Town	Sullivan/Windsor	NH-10-09/VT-14-14
Bayless (1877)	MKP	Sullivan	NH-10-10
Green Sergeants (1866)	Queen	Hunterdon	NJ-10-01
Waldbillig (1955)	Warren	Albany	NY-01-01
Munson (1991)	Queen	Broome	NY-04-02
Downsville (1854)	Long/Queen	Delaware	NY-13-01
Fitches (1870)	Town	Delaware	NY-13-02
Hamden (1859)	Long	Delaware	NY-13-03
Tuscarora Club/Demis (1870)	King	Delaware	NY-13-05
Campbell (1877)	Town	Delaware	NY-13-07
Erpf (1964)	Town	Delaware	NY-13-08
Jay (1857)	Howe	Essex	NY-16-01
Eagle Mills (1967)	Town	Fulton	NY-18-01
Salisbury Center (1875)	MKP/arch	Herkimer	NY-22-01
Frontenac/N. Country (1979)	Town	Jefferson	NY-23-01
Americana Village (1968)	Warren	Madison	NY-27-01
Hyde Hall (1823)	Burr	Otsego	NY-39-01
Buskirk (1857)	Howe	Rensselaer/Wash.	NY-42-02/58-04
Copeland (1879)	Queen	Saratoga	NY-46-01
Blenheim (1855)	Long/arch	Schoharie	NY-48-01
Ludlow Greens (1990)	Town	Suffolk	NY-52-01
Halls Mills (1912)	Town	Sullivan	NY-53-01
Beaverkill/Conklin (1865)	Town	Sullivan	NY-53-02
Van Tran /Livingston (1860)	Town/arch	Sullivan	NY-53-03
Bendo (1860)	Town	Sullivan	NY-53-04
Newfield (1853)	Town	Tompkins	NY-55-01
Perrine (1844)	Burr	Ulster	NY-56-01
Forge (1906)	King	Ulster	NY-56-02
Olive/Turnwood (1889)	Town	Ulster	NY-56-05
Grants Mills (1902)	Town	Ulster	NY-56-06
Eagleville (1858)	Town	Washington	NY-58-01
Shushan (1858)	Town	Washington	NY-58-02
Rexleigh (1874)	Howe	Washington	NY-58-03
Bunker Hill (1894)	Haupt	Catawba	NC-18-01
Pisgah (c1910)		Randolph	NC-76-01
Harshaville (1855)	MKP/arch	Adams	OH-01-02
Kirker (1890)	MKP	Adams	OH-01-10
Dewey Road/Olin's (1873)	Town	Ashtabula	OH-04-03
Creek Road	Town	Ashtabula	OH-04-05
Middle Road (1868)	Howe	Ashtabula	OH-04-06
Root Road (1868)	Town	Ashtabula	OH-04-09
Benetka Road (1900)	Town/arch	Ashtabula	OH-04-12
Graham Road (1867)	Town	Ashtabula	OH-04-13
South Denmark Road (1868)	Town	Ashtabula	OH-04-14
Doyle Road/Mullen (1876)	Town/arch	Ashtabula	OH-04-16
Eagleville Pizza Parlor (1862)	Town	Ashtabula	OH-04-17A
(see above)	Howe/arch	Ashtabula	OH-04-17B
Mechanicsville (1867)	Howe	Ashtabula	OH-04-18
Harpersfield (1868)	Town	Ashtabula	OH-04-19
Riverdale Road (1874)	Town	Ashtabula	OH-04-22
Warner Hollow (1867)	Town	Ashtabula	OH-04-25
State Road (1983)	Pratt	Ashtabula	OH-04-58
Caine Road (1986)	Pratt	Ashtabula	OH-04-61
Giddings Road (1995)	Pratt	Ashtabula	OH-04-62
Netcher Road (1997)	Haupt/arch	Ashtabula	OH-04-63
Palos (1876)	MKP	Athens	OH-05-01
Kidwell (1880)	Howe	Athens	OH-05-02
Blackwood (1879)	MKP	Athens	OH-05-06
St. Mary's Mem. Pk (1992)	Howe	Auglaize	OH-05-54
Shaeffer/Campbell (1875)	MKP	Belmont	OH-07-05
Brown (1878)	Smith	Brown	OH-08-04
New Hope/Bethel (1878)	Howe/arch	Brown	OH-08-05
McCafferty Road (1877)	Howe	Brown	OH-08-08
Bowman/Eagle Creek (1875)	Smith	Brown	OH-08-18
North Pole Road (1875)	Smith	Brown	OH-08-23
George Miller (1879)	Smith	Brown	OH-08-34
State Line/Gov. Bebb (1868)	Wernwag	Butler	OH-09-02
Black/Pugh's Mill (1868)	Long/Childs	Butler	OH-09-03
Stonelick/Perintown (1878)	Howe	Clermont	OH-13-02
Martinsville (1871)	MKP	Clinton	OH-14-09
Lynchburg (1870)	Long	Clinton/Highland	OH-14-11/36-06
Sells/Roller Mill (1995)	MKP	Columbiana	OH-15-01 #2
McClellan (1879)	MKP	Columbiana	OH-15-02
Teegarden/Centennial (1875)	MKP	Columbiana	OH-15-05
Church Hill Road (1875)	MKP	Columbiana	OH-15-08
Thomas J. Malone (1865)	MKP	Columbiana	OH-15-96
Helmick (1996)	MKP	Coshocton	OH-16-02 #2
Chambers Road (1883)	Childs	Delaware	OH-21-04
Hizey/Visintine (1891)	MKP/Queen	Fairfield	OH-23-07
Jon Bright No. 2 (1881)	Bowstring/arch	Fairfield	OH-23-10
Hannaway (1901)	MKP	Fairfield	OH-23-15
Johnston (1887)	Howe	Fairfield	OH-23-16
Zeller/Smith (1906)	MKP/Queen	Fairfield	OH-23-19
Shade/Waterloo (1871)	Burr	Fairfield	OH-23-20
McCleery (1864)	MKP	Fairfield	OH-23-25
Shryer (1891)	MKP	Fairfield	OH-23-27
Charles Holliday (1897)	MKP	Fairfield	OH-23-30
R.F. Baker (1871)	MKP	Fairfield	OH-23-33
Jon Raab (1891)	Queen	Fairfield	OH-23-37
Hartman No. 2 (1888)	Queen	Fairfield	OH-23-38
Mink Hollow (1887)	MKP	Fairfield	OH-23-43
Rock Mill (1901)	Queen	Fairfield	OH-23-48
Roley School House (1899)	MKP	Fairfield	OH-23-49
Bergstresser/Dietz (1887)	Partridge	Franklin	OH-25-03
Weaver Pk/Franklin (1993)	Town	Franklin	OH-25-147
Brannon/Wesner (1885)	MKP	Franklin	OH-25-65
Cemetery Road (1886)	Howe	Greene	OH-29-01
West Engle Mill Rd (1877)	Smith	Greene	OH-29-03
Stevenson Road (1877)	Smith	Greene	OH-29-15
Charleton Mill Road (1883)	Howe	Greene	OH-29-16
Ballard Road (1883)	Howe	Greene	OH-29-18
Indian Camp	MKP	Guernsey	OH-30-04
Armstrong/Cleo (1849)	MKP	Guernsey	OH-30-12
Jediah Hill/Groff Mill (1850)	Queen	Hamilton	OH-31-01
Skull Fork	MKP	Harrison	OH-34-19
JohnsonRd./Petersbg (1870)	Smith	Jackson	OH-40-06
Byer (1872)	Smith	Jackson	OH-40-08
Buckeye Furnace (1871	Smith	Jackson	OH-40-11
Scottown (1877)	MKP (mod)	Lawrence	OH-44-05
Belle Hall (1879)	MKP	Licking	OH-45-01
Boy Scout/Rainrock	MKP	Licking	OH-45-04
Girl Scout/Mercer (1879)	MKP	Licking	OH-45-05
Gregg/Handel (1881)	MKP	Licking	OH-45-06
Canal Greenway (1992)	Town	Licking	OH-45-160
McLain/Lobdell Park (1871)	MKP	Licking	OH-45-17
Davis Farm (1947)	MKP	Licking	OH-45-25
McColly (1876)	Howe	Logan	OH-46-01
Bickham (1877)	Howe	Logan	OH-46-03
Eldean (1860)	Long	Miami	OH-55-01
Foraker (1886)	MKP	Monroe	OH-56-14
Long/Knowlton (1887)	MKP/arch	Monroe	OH-56-18
Germantown (1865)	Bowstring	Montgomery	OH-57-01
Feedwire/Carillon (1870)	Warren/arch	Montgomery	OH-53-37
Jasper Road/Mud Lick (1869)	Warren/arch	Montgomery	OH-57-36
Barkhurst Mill (1872)	MKP/arch	Morgan	OH-58-15
Rosseau	MKP	Morgan	OH-58-32
Helmic/Island Run (1867)	MKP	Morgan	OH-58-35
Adams/SanToy (1875)	MKP	Morgan	OH-58-38
Milton/Campsite (c1920)	MKP	Morgan	OH-58-41
Johnsonl/Salt Crk (1876)	Warren	Muskingum	OH-60-31
Manchester/C. Wiley (1915)	MKP	Noble	OH-61-33
Parrish (1914)	MKP	Noble	OH-61-34
Park Hill/Rich Valley	MKP	Noble	OH-61-40
Huffman Wood	MKP	Noble	OH-61-57
Parks/South (1883)	MKP	Perry	OH-64-02
Hopewell Church (1874)	MKP	Perry	OH-64-03
Jacks Hollow (1879)	MKP	Perry	OH-64-05
Bowmanl/Redington (1859)	MKP	Perry	OH-64-06
Mary Ruffner/Moore (1875)	Smith	Perry	OH-64-84
Valentine/Bill Green (1872)	MKP	Pickaway	OH-65-15
Harshman (1894)	Childs	Preble	OH-68-03
Dixon Branch (1887)	Childs	Preble	OH-68-04
Roberts (1829)	Burr DB	Preble	OH-68-05
Brubaker (1887)	Childs	Preble	OH-68-06
Tyler/Sloane (1891)	Childs	Preble	OH-68-10
Christman (1895)	Childs	Preble	OH-68-12
Geeting (1894)	Childs	Preble	OH-68-13
Warnke (1895)	Childs	Preble	OH-68-14
Buckskin (1873)	Smith	Ross	OH-71-02
Mull (1842)	Town	Sandusky	OH-72-01
Otway (1874)	Smith/arch	Scioto	OH-73-15
Everett Road (1870)	Smith	Summit	OH-77-01 #2
Newton Falls (1831)	Town	Trumbull	OH-78-01
Pottersburg/Up.Darby (1868)	Partridge	Union	OH-80-01
Spain Creek (1870)	Partridge	Union	OH-80-02
Treacle/Winget Rd. (1868)	Partridge	Union	OH-80-03
Axe Handle./Bigelow (1873)	Partridge/arch	Union	OH-80-04
Mt. Olive/Grand Staff (1875)	Queen	Vinton	OH-82-04
Bay/Tinker (1876)	MKP Dbl	Vinton	OH-82-05
Geer Mill/Humpback (1874)	MKP D/arch	Vinton	OH-82-06
Eakin Mill/Arbaugh (1870)	MKP D/arch	Vinton	OH-82-07
Cox (1884)	Queen	Vinton	OH-80-10
Shinn (1886)	MKP/arch	Washington	OH-84-03
Henry (1894)	MKP	Washington	OH-84-06
Root/Qualey (1878)	Long	Washington	OH-84-08
Harra (1878)	Long	Washington	OH-84-11
Bell (1888)	MKP	Washington	OH-84-12
Mill Branch	MKP	Washington	OH-84-17
Schwenderman (1894)	MKP	Washington	OH-84-20
Hills/Hildreth (1878)	Howe	Washington	OH-84-24
Hune (1879)	Long	Washington	OH-84-27
Rinard (1876)	Smith	Washington	OH-84-28
Parker (1876)	Howe	Wyandot	OH-88-03
Swartz (1880)	Howe	Wyandot	OH-88-05
Harris (c1929)	Howe	Benton	OR-02-04
Hayden (1918)	Howe	Benton	OR-02-05
Irish Bend (1954)	Howe	Benton	OR-02-09
Sandy Creek (1921)	Howe	Coos	OR-06-09
Krewson/Pass Creek (1925)	Howe	Douglas	OR-10-02
Rochester (1933)	Howe	Douglas	OR-10-04
Cavitt Creek (1943)	Howe	Douglas	OR-10-06
Neal Lane (1929)	King	Douglas	OR-10-07
Roaring Camp (1929)	Howe	Douglas	OR-10-11
Horse Creek (1930)	Howe	Douglas	OR-10-14
Antelope Creek (1922)	Queen	Jackson	OR-15-02
Lost Creek (1919)	Queen	Jackson	OR-15-03
Wimer (1927)	Queen	Jackson	OR-15-05
McKee (1917)	Howe	Jackson	OR-15-06
Sunny Valley (1920)	Howe	Josephine	OR-17-01
Coyote Creek (1922)	Howe	Lane	OR-20-02
Wildcat (1925)	Howe	Lane	OR-20-04
Lake Crk/Nelson Crk (1928)	Howe	Lane	OR-20-06
Goodpasture (1938)	Howe	Lane	OR-20-10
Belknap (1966)	Howe	Lane	OR-20-11
Pengra (1928)	Howe	Lane	OR-20-15
Unity (1936)	Howe	Lane	OR-20-17
Lowell (1945)	Howe	Lane	OR-20-18
Parvin 1921)	Howe	Lane	OR-20-19
Currin (1925)	Howe	Lane	OR-20-22
Dorena/Star (1949)	Howe	Lane	OR-20-23
Mosby Creek (1920)	Howe	Lane	OR-20-27
Stewart (1930)	Howe	Lane	OR-20-28
Earnest/Russell (1938)	Howe	Lane	OR-20-35
Wendling (1938)	Howe	Lane	OR-20-36
Deadwood (1932)	Howe	Lane	OR-20-38
Office (1944)	Howe	Lane	OR-20-39
Chambers R/R (1936)	Howe	Lane	OR-20-40
Centennial (1987)	Howe	Lane	OR-20-41
Chitwood (1930)	Howe	Lincoln	OR-21-03
Yachats River (1938)	Howe	Lincoln	OR-21-08
Fisher School (1919)	Howe	Lincoln	OR-21-11
Upper Drift Creek (1914)	Howe	Lincoln	OR-21-14
Hannah (1936)	Howe	Linn	OR-22-02
Shimanek (1966)	Howe	Linn	OR-22-03
Gilkey (1939)	Howe	Linn	OR-22-04
Devaney/Weddle (1937)	Howe	Linn	OR-22-05
Larwood (1939)	Howe	Linn	OR-22-06
Hoffman (1936)	Howe	Linn	OR-22-08
Short/Cascadia (1945)	Howe	Linn	OR-22-09
Crawfordsville (1932)	Howe	Linn	OR-22-15
Dohlenburg/Holley (1989)	Howe	Linn	OR-22-17
Gallon House (1916)	Howe	Marion	OR-24-01
Jordan (1937)	Howe	Marion	OR-24-02
Ritner Creek (1927)	Howe	Polk	OR-27-01
Alva 'Doc' Fourtner (1922)	Queen	Polk	OR-27-03
Sauck's/Sachs (1854)	Town	Adams	PA-01-01
Anderson Farm/Reeser	Burr	Adams	PA-01-05
Jack's Mountain (1890)	Burr	Adams	PA-01-08
Heike (1892)	Burr	Adams	PA-01-14
Felton Mill (1892)	Burr	Bedford	PA-05-03
Heirline/Kinton (1902)	Burr	Bedford	PA-05-11
Claycomb (1884)	Burr	Bedford	PA-05-12
Halls Mill (1995)	Burr	Bedford	PA-05-15 #2
Knisley (1867)	Burr	Bedford	PA-05-16
Ryot (1868)	Burr	Bedford	PA-05-17
Cuppett/New Paris (1882)	Burr	Bedford	PA-05-18
Diehl/Turner (1892)	Burr	Bedford	PA-05-19
Palo Alto/Fichtner (1890)	MKP	Bedford	PA-05-21
Bowser/Osterburg (1890)	Burr	Bedford	PA-05-22
Snooks (1880)	Burr	Bedford	PA-05-23
Colvin (1880)	MKP	Bedford	PA-05-24
Jackson Mill (1889)	Burr	Bedford	PA-05-25
Hewitt (1879)	Burr	Bedford	PA-05-26

Pleasantville (1856)	Burr	Berks	PA-06-01
Greisemer's Mill (1832)	Burr	Berks	PA-06-03
Kutz Mill/Sacony (1854)	Burr	Berks	PA-06-05
Wertz/Red (1869)	Burr	Berks	PA-06-06
Dreibelbis Station (1869)	Burr	Berks	PA-06-07
Knapp's (1853)	Burr	Bradford	PA-08-01
Knecht's/Sleifer's (1873)	Town	Bucks	PA-09-02
Van Sant (1875)	Town	Bucks	PA-09-03
Erwinna (1871)	Town	Bucks	PA-09-04
South Perkasie (1832)	Town	Bucks	PA-09-05
Sheard's Mill (1873)	Town	Bucks	PA-09-06
Mood's (1873)	Town	Bucks	PA-09-07
Uhlerstown (1832)	Town	Bucks	PA-09-08
Frankenfield (1872)	Town	Bucks	PA-09-09
Cabin Run (1874)	Town	Bucks	PA-09-10
Loux (1874)	Town	Bucks	PA-09-11
Iron Hill/Pine Valley (1842)	Town	Bucks	PA-09-12
Harrity/Bucks (1841)	MKP	Carbon	PA-13-01
Little Gap (1860)	Burr	Carbon	PA-13-02
Rudolph/Arthur (1886)	Burr	Chester	PA-15-01
Glen Hope (1889)	Burr	Chester	PA-15-02
Linton Stevens (1886)	Burr	Chester	PA-15-03
Speakman No. 1 (1881)	Burr	Chester	PA-15-05
Speakman No. 2 (1881)	Queen	Chester	PA-15-06
Hayes Clark (1971)	Queen	Chester	PA-15-07 #2
Gibson/Harmony Hill (1872)	Burr	Chester	PA-15-10
Larkin (1881)	Burr	Chester	PA-15-11
Sheeder/Hall (1850)	Burr	Chester	PA-15-12
Kennedy (1988)	Burr	Chester	PA-15-13 #2
Rapp's (1866)	Burr	Chester	PA-15-14
Knox/Valley Forge (1865)	Burr	Chester	PA-15-15
Bartram/Goshen (1860)	Burr	Chester/Delaware	PA-15-17/23-02
Mercer (1860)	Burr	Chester/Delaware	PA-15-19
Pine Grove (1884)	Burr	Chester/Delaware	PA-15-22/36-41
McGee's Mills (1873)	Burr	Clearfield	PA-17-01
Logan Mills (1874)	Queen	Clinton	PA-18-01
Fowlersville/Briar (1886)	Queen	Columbia	PA-19-05
Shoemaker (1881)	Queen	Columbia	PA-19-06
Sam Eckman (1876)	Queen	Columbia	PA-19-08
Josiah Hess/Laubach (1875)	Burr	Columbia	PA-19-10
East Paden (1850)	Queen	Columbia	PA-19-11
West Paden (1850	Burr	Columbia	PA-19-12
Snyder (1876)	Burr	Columbia	PA-19-14
Wagner (1856)	Queen	Columbia	PA-19-15
Davis (1875)	Burr	Columbia	PA-19-16
Wanich (1884)	Burr	Columbia	PA-19-18
Esther Furnace (1882)	Queen	Columbia	PA-19-20
Stillwater (1849)	Burr	Columbia	PA-19-21
Kramer (1881)	Queen	Columbia	PA-19-23
Jud Christian (1876)	Queen	Columbia	PA-19-25
Patterson (1845)	Burr	Columbia	PA-19-26
Paar's Mill (1865)	Burr	Columbia	PA-19-29
Krickbaum (1876)	Queen	Col./Northumberland	PA-19-32
Rupert (1847)	Burr	Columbia	PA-19-33
Hollingshead (1850)	Burr	Columbia	PA-19-34
Creasyville (1881)	Queen	Columbia	PA-19-36
Johnson (1882)	Queen	Columbia	PA-19-37
Lawrence L. Knoebel (1876)	Queen	Col./Northumberland	PA-19-39/49-13
Richards/Reichard (1875)	Queen	Col./Northumberland	PA-19-41/49-07
Paperdale	Queen	Columbia	PA-19-46
Ramp (1882)	Burr	Cumberland	PA-21-11
Stoner/Bowmansdale (1862)	Burr	Cumberland/York	PA-21-13/67-04
Henninger Farm	Burr	Dauphin	PA-22-11
Keepville/Sherman (1873)	MKP	Erie	PA-25-02
Gudgeonville (1868)	MKP	Erie	PA-25-03
Waterford (c1875)	Town	Erie	PA-25-04
Martin's Mill Shindle (1849)	Town	Franklin	PA-28-01
Red-Witherspoon (1883)	Burr	Franklin	PA-28-02
Carmichael (1889)	Queen	Greene	PA-30-21
King (1890)	Queen	Greene	PA-30-24
Cox Farm/Lippincott (1940)	King	Greene	PA-30-25
Nettie Wood (1882)	Queen	Greene	PA-30-26
Scott (1885)	Queen	Greene	PA-30-28
Shriver (1900)	Queen	Greene	PA-30-29
White (1919)	Queen	Greene	PA-30-30
Wren's Nest (1993)	King	Greene	PA-30-33
St. Mary's/Shade Gap (1889)	Howe	Huntingdon	PA-31-01
Trusal/Dice (1870)	Town	Indiana	PA-32-03
Hamon (1910)	Town	Indiana	PA-32-04
Kintersburg (1877)	Howe	Indiana	PA-32-05
Thomas (1878)	Town	Indiana	PA-32-06
McCracken (1975)	King	Jefferson	PA-33-03
Academia/Pomeroy (1901)	Burr	Juaniata	PA-34-01
Dimmsville (1902)	Burr	Juaniata	PA-34-02
Oriental/Curry's Crnr (1908)	MKP	Juaniata/Snyder	PA-34-05/55-05
Meiser's Mill (1907)	Burr	Juaniata/Snyder	PA-34-06/55-06
Pool Forge/Wimer (1859)	Burr	Lancaster	PA-36-01
Weaver Mill (1879)	Burr	Lancaster	PA-36-02
Kurtz Mill/Bears Mill (1876)	Burr	Lancaster	PA-36-03
Eberly/Bitzer's Mill (1846)	Burr	Lancaster	PA-36-04
Pinetown/Bushong's (1867)	Burr	Lancaster	PA-36-05
Hunsicker Mill (1975)	Burr	Lancaster	PA-36-06 #2
Red Run/Oberholtz. (1866)	Burr	Lancaster	PA-36-10
Bucher's Mill (1892)	Burr	Lancaster	PA-36-12
Keller/Rettew's Mill (1891)	Burr	Lancaster	PA-36-13
Rosehill/Wenger (1849)	Burr	Lancaster	PA-36-14
Hess Mill/Buck Hill (1844)	Burr	Lancaster	PA-36-15
Landis Mill (1878)	King	Lancaster	PA-36-16
White Rock Forge (1847)	Burr	Lancaster	PA-36-18
Leaman/Eshelman's (1894)	Burr	Lancaster	PA-36-20
Herr/Soudersburg (1885)	Burr	Lancaster	PA-36-21
Neff's Mill (1875)	Burr	Lancaster	PA-36-22
Lime Valley (1871)	Burr	Lancaster	PA-36-23
Baumgardner Mill (1860)	Burr	Lancaster	PA-36-25
Forry Mill (1969)	Burr	Lancaster	PA-36-28
Shenk Mill (1855)	Burr	Lancaster	PA-36-30
Jacob Shearer (1856)	Burr	Lancaster	PA-36-31
Kauffman/Sporting (1874)	Burr	Lancaster	PA-36-32
Jackson Sawmill (1878)	Burr	Lancaster	PA-36-33
Erb's (1887)	Burr	Lancaster	PA-36-34
Risser Mill/Horst (1849)	Burr	Lancaster	PA-36-36
Moore's Mill/Seigrist (1885)	Burr	Lancaster	PA-36-37
Willows (1962)	Burr	Lancaster	PA-36-43
Colemanville No. 2 (1992)	Burr	Lancaster	PA-36-55
McConnell's Mill (1874)	Howe	Lawrence	PA-37-01
Bank's (1889)	Burr	Lawrence	PA-37-02
Bogert (1841)	Burr	Lehigh	PA-39-01
Wehr (1841)	Burr	Lehigh	PA-39-02
Manassas Guth (1858)	Burr	Lehigh	PA-39-03
Rex (1858)	Burr	Lehigh	PA-39-04
Geiger (1858)	Burr	Lehigh	PA-39-05
Schlicher (1882)	Burr	Lehigh	PA-39-06
Bittenbender (1882)	Queen	Luzerne	PA-40-01
Buttonwood (1898)	MKP/Queen	Lycoming	PA-41-01
Cogan House (1877)	Burr	Lycoming	PA-41-02
Fraser/Moreland	Burr	Lycoming	PA-42-03
Kidd's Mill (1869)	Smith	Mercer	PA-43-01
Sam Wagner/Brown (1881)	Burr	Montour/Northumb.	PA-47-01/49-11
Keefer (1853)	Burr	Montour	PA-47-03
Solt's/Kreidersville (1840)	Burr	Northhampton	PA-48-01
Keefer's Station (1888)	Burr	Northumberland	PA-49-02
Rishel (1830)	Burr	Northumberland	PA-49-05
Rebuck/Himmel (1983)	MKP	Northumberland	PA-49-06 #2
Mertz (1976)	King	Northumberland	PA-49-14
Bistline/Flickinger (1871)	Burr	Perry	PA-50-03
Adair/Cisna Mill (1884)	Burr	Perry	PA-50-04
Red/Liverpool (1886)	Burr V	Perry	PA-50-06
Saville (1903)	Burr	Perry	PA-50-07
Kochenderfer (1919)	Burr V	Perry	PA-50-09
Rice/Landisburg (1869)	Burr	Perry	PA-50-10
New Germantown (1891)	Burr	Perry	PA-50-11
Mt. Pleasant (1918)	Burr	Perry	PA-50-12
Book's/Kaufman (1884)	Burr	Perry	PA-50-13
Enslow/Turkey Tail (1904)	Burr	Perry	PA-50-14
Waggoner's Mill (1889)	Burr	Perry	PA-50-15
Dellville (1889)	Burr	Perry	PA-50-16
Fleisher's (1887)	Burr	Perry	PA-50-17
Clay/Wahneta (1890)	Burr	Perry	PA-50-18
Thomas Mill (1855)	Howe	Philadelphia	PA-51-01
Zimmerman (1880)	Burr	Schuylkill	PA-54-01
Rock (1870)	Burr	Schuylkill	PA-54-02
Beavertown/Dreese (1870)	Burr	Snyder	PA-55-02
Klinepeter/Overflow (1871)	Burr	Snyder	PA-55-03
Aline/Meiserville (1884)	Burr	Snyder	PA-55-04
Burkholder/Beechdale (1870)	Burr	Somerset	PA-56-01
Packsaddle (1870)	MKP	Somerset	PA-56-02
Barronvale (1902)	Burr	Somerset	PA-56-03
Cox Crk/Walter's (1859)	Burr	Somerset	PA-56-05
King's (1906)	Burr	Somerset	PA-56-06
Glessner (1880)	Burr	Somerset	PA-56-08
Trostletown/Kantner (1845)	MKP/Queen	Somerset	PA-56-10
Shaffer/Ben's Creek (1877)	Burr	Somerset	PA-56-11
L. Humbert/Faidley (1891)	Burr	Somerset	PA-56-12
Forksville (1850)	Burr	Sullivan	PA-57-01
Hillsgrove/Rinker (1850)	Burr	Sullivan	PA-57-02
Sonestown/Davidson (1850)	Burr	Sullivan	PA-57-03
Old Mill/L.C. Bevan (1850)	Town	Susquehanna	PA-58-01
Millmont/Glen Iron (1855)	Burr	Union	PA-60-01
Hayes (1882)	MKP	Union	PA-60-02
Hassenplug (1825)	Burr	Union	PA-60-03
Factory/Horsham (1880)	Burr	Union	PA-60-04
Hubler Road (1850)	MKP	Union	PA-60-05
Gordon Hufnagle (1981)	Town	Union	PA-60-06
Sprowls (1875)	King	Washington	PA-63-03
Bailey (1889)	Burr	Washington	PA-63-08
Brownlee/Stout	King	Washington	PA-63-09
Crawford	Queen	Washington	PA-63-10
Danley	Queen	Washington	PA-63-11
Day (1875)	Queen	Washington	PA-63-12
McClurg/Devils Den	King	Washington	PA-63-13
Ebenezer Church	Queen	Washington	PA-63-14
Erskine (1845)	Queen	Washington	PA-63-15
Henry (1881)	Queen	Washington	PA-63-16
Hughes (1889)	Queen	Washington	PA-63-17
Jackson's Mill	Queen	Washington	PA-63-18
Krepp's	King	Washington	PA-63-19
Leatherman	Queen	Washington	PA-63-20
Lyle	Queen	Washington	PA-63-21
Longdon/Miller	Queen	Washington	PA-63-22
May/Blaney (1882)	Queen	Washington	PA-63-23
Planto (1876)	King	Washington	PA-63-26
Ralston/Freeman (1915)	King	Washington	PA-63-27
Wilson (1889)	Queen	Washington	PA-63-28
Wyit Sprowls	Queen	Washington	PA-63-29
Wright/Cerl	King	Washington	PA-63-30
Sawhill (1915)	Queen	Washington	PA-63-34
Pine Bank (1870)	King	Washington	PA-63-35
Bells Mills (1850)	Burr	Westmoreland	PA-65-01
Campbell (1909)	Howe	Greenville	SC-23-02
Elizabethton (1882)	Howe	Carter	TN-10-01
Bible/Chucky (1922)	Queen	Greene	TN-30-01
Port Royal (1977)	Howe	Montgomery	TN-63-01 #2
Parks Farm (1910)	King	Obion	TN-66-01
Harrisburg (1875)	Queen	Sevier	TN-78-01
Winnie (1992)	Town	San Augustine	TX-203-01
Station/Salisbury (1865)	Town	Addison	VT-01-01
Hollow/Old Covered (1850)	Town	Addison	VT-01-02
Halpin (1850)	Town	Addison	VT-01-03
Pulp Mill (c1820)	Burr DB	Addison	VT-01-04
East Shoreham RR (1897)	Howe	Addison	VT-01-05
Bridge at the Green (1852)	Town	Bennington	VT-02-01
Henry (1989)	Town	Bennington	VT-02-02
Papermill Village (1889)	Town	Bennington	VT-02-03
Silk Road/Locust (1840)	Town	Bennington	VT-02-04
Chiselville (1870)	Town	Bennington	VT-02-05
Greenbank Hollow (1886)	Queen	Caledonia	VT-03-01
Schoolhouse/Chase (1879)	Queen	Caledonia	VT-03-03
Chamberlain (1881)	Queen	Caledonia	VT-03-04
Sanborn (1867)	Paddleford	Caledonia	VT-03-05
Millers Run/Bradley (1995)	Queen	Caledonia	VT-03-06
Randall/Burrington (1865)	Queen	Caledonia	VT-03-07
Lake Shore (1898)	Tied arch	Chittenden	VT-04-01
Upper/Sequin (1849)	Burr	Chittenden	VT-04-02
Quinlan/Lower (1849)	Burr	Chittenden	VT-04-03
Westford (1837)	Burr	Chittenden	VT-04-05
Cambridge Village (1845)	Burr DD	Chittenden	VT-04-06
Hopkins (1875)	Town	Franklin	VT-06-01
Village/Maple Street (1865)	Town	Franklin	VT-06-02
East Fairfield (1865)	Queen	Franklin	VT-06-03
Comstock (1883)	Town	Franklin	VT-06-04
Fuller/Black Falls (1890)	Town	Franklin	VT-06-05
Hectorville (1883)	Town/King	Franklin	VT-06-06
Hutchins (1883)	Town	Franklin	VT-06-07
Longley/Harnois (1863)	Town	Franklin	VT-06-08
Creamery/West Hill (1883)	Town	Franklin	VT-06-09
Scott/Grist Mill (1872)	Burr	Lamoille	VT-08-01
Poland/Station (1887)	Burr	Lamoille	VT-08-02
Little/Gates Farm (1897)	Burr	Lamoille	VT-08-04 #2
Lumber Mill (1890)	Queen	Lamoille	VT-08-06
Morgan (1887)	Queen	Lamoille	VT-08-07
Power House (1870)	Queen	Lamoille	VT-08-08
Scribner	Queen	Lamoille	VT-08-09
Red/Sterling (1869)	King	Lamoille	VT-08-11
Stowe Hollow (c1900)	Queen	Lamoille	VT-08-12
Village/Church St. (c1877)	Queen	Lamoille	VT-08-13
Montgomery (1887)	Queen	Lamoille	VT-08-14
Jaynes/Codding (c1877)	Queen	Lamoille	VT-08-15
Fisher R/R (1908)	Town	Lamoille	VT-08-16
Moxley/Guy (1883)	Queen	Orange	VT-09-01
Kingsbury/Hyde (1904)	MKP	Orange	VT-09-02
Gifford/C.K. Smith (1904)	MKP	Orange	VT-09-03
Blaisdell (1904)	MKP	Orange	VT-09-04
Union Village (1867)	MKP	Orange	VT-09-05
Sayres	Haupt/arch	Orange	VT-09-06
Howe (1879)	MKP	Orange	VT-09-07

Cilley/Lower (1883)	MKP	Orange	VT-09-08
Mill/Hayward&Noble (1883)	MKP	Orange	VT-09-09
Larkin (1902)	MKP	Orange	VT-09-10
Flint (1874)	Queen	Orange	VT-09-11
Orne (1881)	Paddleford	Orleans	VT-10-01
Coventry (1881)	Paddleford	Orleans	VT-10-02
River Road/School (c1885)	Town	Orleans	VT-10-03
Sanderson (1838)	Town	Rutland	VT-11-02
Kingsley Mill (1836)	Town	Rutland	VT-11-03
Gorham/Goodnough (1842)	Town	Rutland	VT-11-04
Hammond (1843)	Town	Rutland	VT-11-05
Depot (1853)	Town	Rutland	VT-11-06
Cooley (1849)	Town	Rutland	VT-11-07
Brown (1880)	Town	Rutland	VT-11-09
Twin (1850)	Town	Rutland	VT-11-10
Coburn/Cemetery (1851)	Queen	Washington	VT-12-02
Orton Farm/Martin (1890)	Queen	Washington	VT-12-06
Moseley (1899)	King	Washington	VT-12-07
Station/Northfield (1872)	Town	Washington	VT-12-08
Slaughter House	Queen	Washington	VT-12-09
Lower/Newell (1872)	Queen	Washington	VT-12-10
Upper	Queen	Washington	VT-12-11
Pine Brook (1872)	King	Washington	VT-12-12
Village (1833)	Burr	Washington	VT-12-14
Warren (1880)	Queen	Washington	VT-12-15
Robbins Nest (1965)	Queen	Washington	VT-12-18
A.M. Foster (1980)	Queen	Washington	VT-12-75
Creamery (1879)	Town	Windham	VT-13-01
West Dummerston (1872)	Town	Windham	VT-13-02
Kidder Hill (1870)	King	Windham	VT-13-03
Green River (1873)	Town	Windham	VT-13-04
Williamsville (1870)	Town	Windham	VT-13-05
Hall (1982)	Town	Windham	VT-13-07 #2
Worrall (1868)	Town	Windham	VT-13-10
Bartonsville (1871)	Town	Windham	VT-13-11
Scott (1870)	Town/King	Windham	VT-13-13
Victorian Village (1967)	King	Windham	VT-13-23
Martin's Mill (1881)	Town	Windsor	VT-14-01
Willard	Town	Windsor	VT-14-02
Baltimore (1870)	Town	Windsor	VT-14-03
Stoughton/Titcomb (1880)	MKP	Windsor	VT-14-04
Salmond (c1875)	MKP	Windsor	VT-14-05
Up. Falls/Downer's (1851)	Town	Windsor	VT-14-08
Best (1890)	Tied/arch	Windsor	VT-14-10
Bowers/Brownsville	Tied/arch	Windsor	VT-14-11
Taftsville (1836)	MKP/arch	Windsor	VT-14-12
Lincoln (1877)	Pratt/arch	Windsor	VT-14-13
Middle/Union Street (1969)	Town	Windsor	VT-14-15
Twigg/Smith (1870)	Town	Windsor	VT-14-17
South Pomfret (1870)	Town	Windsor	VT-14-18
Humpback (1857)	MKP	Alleghany	VA-03-01
Marysville (1878)	Howe	Campbell	VA-16-01
Sinking Creek (1916)	Queen	Giles	VA-35-01
Link Farm (1912)	Queen	Giles	VA-35-02
Red Maple/Craig (1919)	Queen	Giles	VA-35-03
Old German (1974)	King	James City	VA-47-01
Bob White/Lower (1920)	Queen	Patrick	VA-68-01
Jack's Creek/Upper (1916)	Queen	Patrick	VA-68-02
Biedler Farm (c1800)	Burr	Rockingham	VA-79-01
Meems Bottom (1979)	Burr	Shenandoah	VA-82-01
Milbrandt (1976)	King	Clark	WA-06-01
Grist Mill (1994)	Queen	Clark	WA-06-02
Schafer Farm (1966)	Howe	Grays Harbor	WA-14-01
Peéll (1934)	Howe	Lewis	WA-21-02
Grays River (1989)	Howe	Wahkiakum	WA-35-02 #2
Colfax/Road (1922)	Howe	Whitman	WA-38-01
Philippi (1852)	Long/arch DB	Barbour	WV-01-01
Carrolton (1855)	Burr	Barbour	WV-01-02
Milton/Sinks Mill (1876)	Howe	Cabell	WV-06-01
Center Point (1888)	Long	Doddridge	WV-09-01
Herns Mill (1884)	Queen	Greenbrier	WV-13-01
Hokes Mill (1899)	Long	Greenbrier	WV-13-02
Fletcher (1891)	MKP	Harrison	WV-17-03
Simpson Crk/Hollen (1881)	MKP	Harrison	WV-17-12
Sarvis Fk/Sandyville (1889)	Long/arch	Jackson	WV-18-01
Staats Mill (1888)	Long	Jackson	WV-18-04
Old Red/Walkersville (1902)	Queen	Lewis	WV-21-03
Barrackville (1853)	Burr	Marion	WV-25-02
Dents Run/Laurel P. (1889)	MKP	Monongalia	WV-31-03
Laurel Crk/Lillydale (1911)	Queen	Monroe	WV-32-01
Indian Creek (1898)	Long	Monroe	WV-32-02
Denmar/Locust Creek (1888)	DblWarren	Pocahontas	WV-38-01
Hundred/Fish Creek (1881)	MKP	Wetzel	WV-52-01
Stonefield Village (1962)	Howe	Grant	WI-22-01
Cedarburg (1876)	Town	Ozaukee	WI-46-01
Chequamegon (1991)	Town	Price	WI-51-01
Red Mill (1971)	Town	Waupaca	WI-69-01
Ashnola River Road (1923)	Howe	Similkameen Div.	BC-01-01
Bamford Colpitts (1943)	Burr	Albert	NB-01-01
Crooked Crk #3 (1945)	Howe	Albert	NB-01-03
Lower Forty Five #1 (1914)	Howe	Albert	NB-01-04
Point Wolfe (1992)	Howe	Albert	NB-01-05 #2
P.Jonah/Turtle Crk #4 (1912)	Burr	Albert	NB-01-07
Germantown Lk (1903)	Howe	Albert	NB-01-08
H.Steeves/Weldon #3 (1923)	Howe	Albert	NB-01-11
Sawmill Creek # 1 (1905)	Howe	Albert	NB-01-20
William Mitton (1942)	Burr	Albert	NB-01-22
Adair/N. Becag.#1(1948)	Howe	Carleton	NB-02-01
Ellis/N. Becag. #4 (1909)	Howe	Carleton	NB-02-05
Florenceville (1906)	Howe	Carleton	NB-02-06
Hartland (1921)	Howe	Carleton	NB-02-07
Keenen (1927)	Howe	Carleton	NB-02-08
Mangrum (1909)	Howe	Carleton	NB-02-10
Benton/Eel River #3 (1927)	Howe	Carleton/York	NB-02-15/15-12
Canal (1917)	Howe	Charlotte	NB-03-01
Dumbarton (1928)	Howe	Charlotte	NB-03-02
Flume Ridge (1905)	Burr	Charlotte	NB-03-03
Maxwell Crossing (1910)	Howe	Charlotte	NB-03-04
McGuire (1913)	Howe	Charlotte	NB-03-05
Mill Pond (1910)	Howe	Charlotte	NB-03-06
McCann (1938)	Howe	Charlotte	NB-03-09
Tom Graham (1928)	Howe	Kent	NB-05-03
St. Nicholas R. #1 (1919)	Howe	Kent	NB-05-08
Cameron's Mill (1950)	Howe	Kent	NB-05-12
Bloomfield Creek (1917)	Howe	Kings	NB-06-01
Centreville Mill (1911)	Howe	Kings	NB-06-02
Darlings Island (1914)	Howe	Kings	NB-06-04
French Village (1912)	Howe	Kings	NB-06-05
Malone (1911)	Howe	Kings	NB-06-11
Marven (1903)	Howe	Kings	NB-06-12
Macfarlane (1909)	Howe	Kings	NB-06-13
Bayswater (1920)	Howe	Kings	NB-06-15
Moore's Mills (1923)	Howe	Kings	NB-06-16
Oldsfield (1910)	Howe	Kings	NB-06-17
Plumweseep (1911)	Howe	Kings	NB-06-18
Trout Creek #4 (1905)	Howe	Kings	NB-06-19
Salmon (1907)	Howe	Kings	NB-06-21
Smithtown (1914)	Howe	Kings	NB-06-24
Tranton (1927)	Howe	Kings	NB-06-26
Bell/Trout Creek #3 (1902)	Howe	Kings	NB-06-28
Moosehorn (1915)	Howe	Kings	NB-06-29
Boniface (1925)	Howe	Madawaska	NB-07-02
Borneault Settlement (1939)	Howe	Madawaska	NB-07-04
Quisibis River #2 (1951)	Howe	Madawaska	NB-07-05
Nelson Hollow (1900)	Howe	Northumberland	NB-08-08
Burpee (1913)	Howe	Queens	NB-09-01
Aaron Clark (1927)	Howe	Queens	NB-09-02
Starkey (1939)	Howe	Queens	NB-09-08
Bayard (1921)	Howe	Queens	NB-09-09
Tynemouth (1927)	Howe	St. John	NB-11-04
Irish River (1935)	Howe	St. John	NB-11-05
Hardscrabble (1946)	Howe	St. John	NB-11-06
Bell (1931)	Howe	Sunbury	NB-12-01
Hoyt Station (1936)	Howe	Sunbury	NB-12-02
Mill Settlement (1912)	Howe	Sunbury	NB-12-03
Patrick Owen (1909)	Howe	Sunbury	NB-12-05
Tomlinson Mill (1918)	Howe	Victoria	NB-13-03
Budd (1913)	Howe	Westmoreland	NB-14-05
Joshua Gallant (1935)	Howe	Westmoreland	NB-14-07
Boudreau (1930)	Howe	Westmoreland	NB-14-08
Hasty (1929)	Howe	Westmoreland	NB-14-09
Poirier (1901)	Howe	Westmoreland	NB-14-12
Wheaton (1916)	Howe	Westmoreland	NB-14-13
Parkindale (1915)	Howe	Westmoreland	NB-14-17
Nackawick Siding (1927)	Howe	York	NB-15-06
Stone Ridge (1914)	Howe	York	NB-15-08
Guelph (1992)	Town	Wellington	ON-52-01
Kissing (1881)	Queen	Waterloo	ON-51-01
Alphonse Normardin (1950)	Town	Abitibi-Est	QC-01-05
Turgeon (1953)	Town	Abitibi-Est	QC-01-07
Laflamme River (1942)	Town	Abitibi-Est	QC-01-18
Panache Creek (1955)	Town	Abitibi-Est	QC-01-21
St. Maurice (1946)	Town	Abitibi-Est	QC-01-22
Laflamme River #2 (1954)	Town	Abitibi-Est	QC-01-25
Tourville Creek (1937)	Town	Abitibi-Est	QC-01-26
Carrier (1955)	Town	Abitibi-Est	QC-01-28
Champagne (1941)	Town	Abitibi-Est	QC-01-29
Laas River (1958)	Town	Abitibi-Est	QC-01-30
Calamité (1927)	Town	Abitibi-Quest	QC-02-04
Bouchard (1927)	Town	Abitibi-Quest	QC-02-05
de Chazel (1935)	Town	Abitibi-Quest	QC-02-11
de Macamic (1930)	Town	Abitibi-Quest	QC-02-13
du Petit Quatre	Town	Abitibi-Quest	QC-02-20
de Ile (1943)	Town	Abitibi-Quest	QC-02-23
Leslie Creek (1943)	Town	Abitibi-Quest	QC-02-32
des Souvenirs (1954)	Town	Abitibi-Quest	QC-02-33
Turgeon (1948)	Town	Abitibi-Quest	QC-02-34
Levasseur (1928)	Town	Abitibi-Quest	QC-02-37
Paradis (1939)	Town	Abitibi-Quest	QC-02-39
Perreault (1908)	Town	Arthabaska	QC-04-06
Descormiers (1904)	King	Arthabaska	QC-04-07
Poisson	Queen	Arthabaska	QC-04-09
Perreault (1928)	Town	Beauce	QC-06-01
Bolduc (1937)	Town	Beauce	QC-06-02
Grandchamp (1883)	Town	Berthier	QC-09-02
St. Edgar (1938)	Town	Bonaventure	QC-10-05
Balthazard (1932)	Town	Brome	QC-11-01
Decelles (1938)	Town	Brome	QC-11-02
Province Hill (1896)	Town	Brome	QC-11-03
Bordeleau (1932)	Town	Champlain	QC-13-03
St. Placide (1926)	Town	Charlevoix	QC-14-03
du Faubourg (1929)	Town	Chicoutimi	QC-17-01
du lac (1934)	Town	Chicoutimi	QC-17-04
Gagnon	Town	Chicoutimi	QC-17-06
Drouin	MKP	Compton	QC-18-01
Eustis (1908)	MKP	Compton	QC-18-02
John Cook (1868)	Town	Compton	QC-18-04
McDermott (1886)	MKP	Compton	QC-18-06
McVetty-McKerry (1893)	Town	Compton	QC-18-08
Wellis-Leggett (1930)	Town	Compton	QC-18-09
Galipeault (1923)	Town	GaspE Nord	QC-23-01
Marois (1933)	Town	Gatineau	QC-25-02
Cousineau (1932)	Town	Gatineau	QC-25-08
de Aigle (1925)	Town	Gatineau	QC-25-11
Ruisseau Meech (1924)	Town	Gatineau	QC-25-12
Barry Kelly (1923)	Town	Gatineau	QC-25-13
Savoyard (1931)	Town	Gatineau	QC-25-15
Powerscourt/Percy (1861)	McCallum	Huntingdon	QC-27-01
Collége/Ouelle (1919)	Town	Kamouraska	QC-32-02
de Ferme Rouge (1903)	Town	Labelle	QC-33-02
de Ferme Rouge (1903)	Town	Labelle River	QC-33-03
Armand Lachaine (1906)	Town	Labelle	QC-33-05
Chem. Annonciation (1904)	Town	Labelle	QC-33-10
Duchame (1946)	Town	Laviolette	QC-37-02
Thiffault (1946)	Town	Laviolette	QC-37-03
du Sault (1943)	Town	Islet	QC-39-01
St. André (1927)	Town	Lotbiniere	QC-40-03
Caron (1933)	Town	Lotbiniere	QC-40-04
Jean Chasse (1945)	Town	Metane	QC-42-01
Belanger (1925)	Town	Metane	QC-42-02
Coulée/Carrier (1936)	Town	Metane	QC-42-03
Pierre/Carrier (1918)	Town	Metane	QC-42-05
Fracois Gagnon (1942)	Town	Metane	QC-42-06
Heppell (1909)	Town	Matapédia	QC-43-02
Routhierville (1931)	Town	Matapédia	QC-43-04
Anse St. Jean (1931)	Town	Matapédia	QC-43-05
Reed Mill (1928)	Town	Megantic	QC-44-01
Lambert (1948)	Town	Megantic	QC-44-08
Guthrie (1845	Town	Missisquoi	QC-45-01
Freeport (c1870)	Town	Missisquoi	QC-45-02
Des Riviéres (1884)	Town	Missisquoi	QC-45-03
Gareau (1944)	Town	Montcalm	QC-46-01
Ste. Lucie (1936)	Town	Montmagny	QC-47-02
des Raymond (1928)	Town	Nicolet	QC-51-01
Philémon Deschenes (1905)	Town	Nicolet	QC-51-03
Marchand (1898)	Town/Queen	Pontiac	QC-53-01
St. Anaclet (1933)	Town	Rimouski	QC-58-03
des Draveurs (1930)	Town	Rimouski	QC-58-04
de al Riviére Hatee (1936)	Town	Rimouski	QC-58-05
Beauséjour (1932)	Town	Rimouski	QC-58-07
Rouge (1936)	Town	Roberval	QC-60-04
Painchaud (1913)	Town	Roberval	QC-60-16
Louis Gravel (1934)	Town	Saguenay	QC-62-01
Baie St. Ludger (c1945)	Town	Saguenay	QC-62-03
St. Mathieu (1936)	Town	St. Maurice	QC-65-01
Cousineau (c1888)	Town	Shefford	QC-66-02
Capelton	Town	Sherbrooke	QC-67-02
Milby	Town	Sherbrooke	QC-67-03
Narrows (1881)	Town	Stanstead	QC-69-03
Landry (1938)	Town	Témiscamingue	QC-70-02
La Loutre/E. Paquin (1933)	Town	Témiscamingue	QC-70-04
St. Jean de la Lande (1940)	Town	Témiscouata	QC-71-03
Prud homme (1918)	Town	Terrebonne	QC-72-01
St. Camille (1933)	Town	Wolfe	QC-75-03
Davitt/Monaghan (1878)	Howe	Drummond	QC-80-01